C0065 66625

D1439076

A FULL BACK SLOWER THAN YOUR AVERAGE PROP

AN AUTOBIOGRAPHY

IAN SMITH

This edition first published in Great Britain in 2019 by

ARENA SPORT
An imprint of Birlinn Limited
West Newington House
10 Newington Road
Edinburgh
EH9 1QS

www.arenasportbooks.co.uk

Copyright © Ian Smith 2019

ISBN: 9781909715813
eBook ISBN: 9781788851824

The right of Ian Smith to be identified as the author
of this work has been asserted by him in accordance with the
Copyright, Designs and Patents Act 1988.

All rights reserved. No part of this publication may be reproduced,
stored or transmitted in any form, or by any means electronic,
mechanical, photocopying, recording or otherwise, without the
express written permission of the publisher.

Every effort has been made to trace copyright holders and obtain their permission for the use of copyright
material. The publisher apologises for any errors or omissions and would be grateful if notified of any
corrections that should be incorporated in future reprints or editions of this book.

British Library Cataloguing-in-Publication Data
A catalogue record for this book is available on request from the British Library.

Designed and typeset by Polaris Publishing, Edinburgh
www.polarispublishing.com

Printed and bound by CPI Group (UK) Ltd, Croydon, CR0 4YY

CONTENTS

*Most of us don't leave much of a mark and we disappear almost completely
when the last person who remembers us also dies*

This book is written for my grandchildren and their children

PROLOGUE

The Magic

It is 9.45 on a Saturday morning in the winter of 1953/54. The temperature is only just above freezing. A little nine-year-old boy is standing, shivering, with the sleeves of his heavy wet blue-and-white striped woollen jersey hanging down over his hands – no vest, no gloves, no second jersey underneath. His shorts are soaked, his socks sodden below knees that are blue and twitching with the cold, and his leather ankle-high boots, with nailed-down studs, are thick with glutinous mud.

The boy is one of fifteen nine-year-olds playing a school match for George Heriot's 36th XV, otherwise known as the 6th Juniors. He is standing in the middle of the most enormous rugby pitch, with a huge grandstand and a massive press box where he and his teammates changed before the match and where they will return, almost hypothermic, an hour hence.

The few parents watching the match do so in silence, as cheering is not encouraged – in fact it is actively banned by Mr Archie McIntyre, the bald-headed tyrant who, along with Mr Donald Hastie, ruled not only the boys' behaviour but that of their parents as well.

'Heriot's parents do not shout or cheer,' one of the masters could be heard to say to a rogue parent who had committed the grievous sin of encouraging their child.

The heavy vertical rain, which shows no sign of stopping, is cascading off the boy's nose and running down the back of his neck. A fog has begun to roll in, largely obscuring the distant try line and making the heavy leather ball even harder to catch or kick. All in all, it is a miserable picture. Yet the little boy is having the time of his life. It is his first game of rugby and all he has ever wanted to do.

I should know — I was that little boy and it is a morning I have never forgotten, even though it happened nearly sixty-five years ago.

INTRODUCTION

I'm sorry to tell you that David Boyd has died.

I must admit that it has been a very emotional experience writing this book, because it has made me examine how I feel about rugby after almost sixty years of either watching, playing, coaching or writing about what I believe to be the greatest of all the team sports.

It is only after you retire from rugby that you begin to appreciate what you took for granted for so long as a player. It might be at the start of the new season, or perhaps after injury prematurely ends your playing days, that you venture back into the changing room only to realise that there is now a barrier between you and the men you may have spent years in the same team as – men you love in an unspoken way, teammates that you would accept injury and pain for without giving it a second thought, men you would spend so much time with that you became like brothers.

People who have never played the game are unlikely to understand the invisible bond that holds a rugby team together.

The instant you retire, however, something goes. You will never again be part of the dressing room humour, the in-joke, the leg-pulling, the snide remark . . . the look. You are out of the loop and you'll never be in it again. You don't feel the pain at first, but all too quickly you become like an addict deprived of his fix, an alcoholic who wants desperately to drink but can't risk even one sip.

This feeling affects former players in different ways. Some can't face watching a match for years or even going to their club for a drink. Others can't bear the smell of liniment or hear the sound of boots on concrete as players emerge from the dressing room without a desperate longing overtaking them. Some take up coaching, but have to leave the dressing room as the players gather together in a huddle and bond before going out to do battle.

These conflicting emotions never leave you, this sense of total frustration. Even when you are old and are crippled with arthritis, you still dream at night of being summoned from the crowd to play, and managing to be the hero of the hour as you seize victory from the jaws of defeat.

Rugby is an incurable addiction. That's why teammates and foes of old have so much in common when given the chance to meet. They relive past glories, catastrophes, incidents on and off the field, memories of matches won and lost that bind them together. In these moments, the barriers come down, the past seems like yesterday, and for a few hours they are transported back to the days when they played, and they are once again in a real rugby environment. Camaraderie may not be the best word to describe what you had, but that is what it was and still is.

For me, it isn't just the smell of liniment or the crack of studs on concrete that takes me back to my rugby-playing days, but also the smell of burning leaves. Burning leaves was the smell of autumn, which meant the rugby season, which I grew to love with a passion that was to totally consume me. Every autumn when I smell burning leaves I feel a heartache, a longing. I can close my eyes and I'm once again running on to a rugby pitch. I hate autumn now.

I hope you will enjoy reading about the highs and the lows of my rugby career, and if you are as I am, an ex-player looking back with your own fond memories, bells may ring, perhaps echoes of your own rugby career may resound. You may even read about yourself, or games you were involved in, because if you are aged between sixty and eighty and played rugby in Scotland, England, Ireland, Wales, France, Germany, Australia, Hong Kong, or Japan, there is every chance you will know people who can be found in this book – or perhaps even find yourself.

If you are a younger reader I want to tell the story of what rugby was like before leagues, substitutes, money, collisions, promising careers cut short by serious injury, coaches, television match officials, artificial pitches, roofs being closed, twenty-three players in a matchday XV . . . It was a time when players could rise from their club 3rd XV to represent their country in a Test match in ten short days. Impossible, you might think – but it happened to me.

In other words, I want to tell you about a time when rugby was fun yet taken incredibly seriously and somehow fitted in around a career. It was a time that still left room for a few beers and some high jinks after a match without the risk of any off-field activity being spotted, recorded and reported because there were no such things as smartphones and social media and the press were interested in the sport and the sport alone.

These are some of the reasons for wanting to write this book. But there is also another one.

'I'm sorry to tell you that David Boyd has died.'

Just before Christmas in 2016 I heard that the man who had been my last rugby captain at school had passed away after a short battle with cancer. His name was David Boyd – to give him his full initials D.S.C. Boyd – and he had been our excellent 1st XV scrum half for two seasons. On receiving the news, a little part of me died as well. To be honest, our paths had rarely crossed after leaving school, but we had shared a bond when we met that is unique amongst rugby players, something totally different to just being friends from our schooldays.

I replied to the sad news by emailing the group I still belong to, based on the school 1st XV in 1961/62, and attached an old press cutting with a photograph featuring David and one or two others in action in a 1st XV match. Shortly afterwards I received a response from another ex-team member who also featured in the photo, saying he didn't know the picture existed, and indeed he had forgotten all about the game that day.

Of course, we often forget events in our lives which were of great significance at the time, and then, when we die, no one remembers – but that seems to me very sad. I then read David's obituary in *The Scotsman* and was astounded to discover he had been awarded a medal for bravery and had become a very successful yachtsman and a very senior banker – very little of which I knew. This got me to thinking about how one-generational our memories are.

Earlier on in 2016, the legendary Alastair Biggar of Scotland and British & Irish Lions fame died after a long battle with cancer, and I realised that he was the third of the four men who got their debut caps for Scotland against South Africa in December 1969 to die.

His passing left me as the only survivor from the new caps that day.

Duncan Patterson and Gordon Brown both died some time before Alastair, and apart from that sobering thought it has made me think of all the personal memories that have died with them.

That was a large part of my decision to write my rugby autobiography – so my grandchildren and great-grandchildren, if they have any interest in rugby at all, will have some idea what part I played in the sport that dominated my life between 1951 and 1983. But it took Julie, my wife, to bring me to book, so to speak, when she found and read the press cuttings my father had begun to lovingly collect of my rugby career over fifty-five years ago. What she said, in effect, was that everything I had told her about my rugby career, in that I hadn't been all that good, about all the luck and good fortune I had happen to me, was in fact rubbish. Everything she had read had been complimentary, so I must have been very good.

I omitted to tell her that my father had made certain that none of the multitude of poor press reports were ever saved! The conversation that night, some five years ago, made me realise that I belong to a lost and very lucky generation of rugby players who have a tale to tell about a rugby career that simply couldn't happen in the modern professional game.

This story describes in detail the nerve-racking journey experienced by that little boy who played for the 36th XV in 1953 as he progressed towards the great honour of representing his country, followed by a slow but enjoyable decline thereafter. It is a window into rugby as it was and, sadly, will never be again. I hope you will enjoy it.

ONE

Mine

As I began preparing to commit myself to print and started looking at the press reports from 1961 when I made my school 1st XV debut it also brought back to me things I had completely forgotten.

As a full back there was the fear as I waited under the first high ball of the season, the first high ball of a match. I prayed that no one ever saw the fear I felt, and that my ability was up to the task in hand of catching that ball and taking whatever tackles and blows came as a result without flinching.

Sadly, this fear was shown by some when moving up a playing level, being chosen for a representative side, and coming under closer scrutiny from the press and the selectors. The question might well be asked, was it better to be brave, stand your ground and drop a high ball, or just not quite be in quite the right place, leaving another to take what was rightfully yours, and thus appearing blameless?

Many promising rugby careers foundered as ex-players turned rugby correspondents soon found you out. They knew whether you were able but chicken, or scared but brave, or saddest of all scared but brave and not good enough. You can, in time, build confidence in yourself as to your ability to stand your ground and catch everything that is thrown at you – but how thin that veneer of confidence can be and how quickly it can be destroyed.

Obviously, I can only write with the experience of my own position as a full back, but every position has its own worries, and whilst my fears always related to the high ball, a prop probably has far bigger concerns – but I made certain I stayed as far away from the front row as I possibly could.

The fear factor, which affects players in completely different ways, is not something you often read about in autobiographies, but as this is my story I need to be honest about how I felt.

Some players need encouragement, always to be told they have done well, or told not to worry because they'll be fine the next time, whilst others need a kick up the backside. I always needed encouraging, especially if I got to the first high ball (which was always a problem as I'd much rather let it bounce) and then dropped it.

To be fair, that did not happen very often. If I plucked up the courage to get underneath it, I almost always caught it.

The call of 'Mine!' or 'My ball!' was something I was taught very early and almost without exception that used to make me get to the ball or stand my ground. What is staggering is how the on-board computer works. The brain has some way of inputting how hard and how high the ball is kicked, what the wind is doing, where the nearest opponents are, and allows a judgement call as to whether you need to call for a mark or not. It all comes about from experience, borne out of years of fielding high balls from childhood, practising, and playing.

I read many rugby autobiographies and most of them are written by world stars of the game, acknowledged by their peers and recognised globally. Increasingly they move between huge clubs like Leicester, Saracens, Wasps and Bath, or they are hired from New Zealand, South Africa, Australia and the Pacific Islands and, more and more like football stars, they move where the money is. Loyalty today seems to be based on cash, so the rugby I will be writing about has long gone. I hate the expression, 'in my day things were different', but I am going to use it here because they were.

Things were certainly very different at the time this story begins. It was only six years after the Second World War had ended.

I was born in Dundee in 1944 but moved to Edinburgh with my parents when I was still very small. When I was five years old I went to George Heriot's School, in September 1949, and there I stayed for the next fourteen years before leaving in 1963.

This was extremely lucky for me because it would have been much easier for my parents to have sent me to George Watson's College which was much closer. Indeed, we could have walked there in fifteen minutes, instead of getting on the number twenty-three tramcar from Morningside into town.

Both Heriot's and Watson's are very famous rugby schools and have played a prominent role in the history of Scottish rugby. Watson's had been, for many years, possibly Heriot's biggest rivals, and like Heriot's has had its fair share of famous rugby former pupils. Little did I think as a five-year-old that I would become the seventh Heriot's full back to play for Scotland.

None of this would have happened had I gone to Watson's. To be fair both schools had one thing in common, and that was the fact that to almost all the boys, rugby was a religion.

With a rugby-mad father, I suspect he had done his homework, and whilst realistically Watson's was the ideal choice, Heriot's probably looked the better bet for him, and thus for me. The truth of the matter I suspect is that I failed the entrance exam for Watson's whereas Heriot's took me on. Whatever the reason, I loved my fourteen years there.

I think the most important moment in a rugby player's life is when and how he or she is introduced to the game. It doesn't necessarily have to be playing, it can be watching that may be just as powerful. In this respect my father played it perfectly.

My father Bill Smith (W.A. Smith), educated at Morgan Academy in Dundee, was a sports fanatic, good enough to be a single figure handicap golfer, a winner of tennis tournaments, and a graduate of St Andrews University where he won a blue for athletics and played rugby for the university. He was very proud to have played in the same university team as the 1938 Lion, Duncan Macrae.

I can't have been more than six when my father took me to my first rugby international at Murrayfield. It was Scotland versus Wales in 1951. Through the school we bought enclosure seats, which were benches right round the ground reserved for school-children. It meant an unbroken view, because apart from the huge west stand, Murrayfield was all terracing at that time.

There are three things I remember about the game. The first was where we were sitting, which was right behind and in line with a Scottish player who dropped a goal. That image has been fixed in my mind ever since, especially when my father told me it was Peter Kininmonth the Scottish number eight. It was unheard of then for a forward to drop a goal, and almost unheard of now, and I hadn't a clue what he had done but everyone stood up and cheered. Wales seemed to crumble after that and Scotland won 19–0.

The second thing was the Scotland full back, who was small, quite plump, had number one on his back (the numbers are reversed now), and he kicked the ball over the bar. I didn't know what penalties and conversions were then, but everyone got very excited, and my father told me that his name was Ian Thomson, that he had gone to Heriot's, had three initials as did I (I.H.M.) and he was only nineteen years old. This was fantastic, and from that moment I wanted to be play for Scotland.

The third thing was the colours and the noise, the fervent singing of the Welsh supporters, especially their national anthem, plus the unique smell everywhere of pipe tobacco. The whole terrace seemed red; my father had taken me down to Princes Street on the morning of the match and it too had been a sea of Welsh red.

There was a story about the aftermath of the 19–0 victory over Wales who were stuffed full of players who had recently toured New Zealand with the Lions in 1950. In fairness they had been the overwhelming favourites to win the match comfortably. On the Sunday after the game, they were taken by coach to see the Forth Bridge, described as one of the modern wonders of the world. When they got out of the coach, a selector said, 'Enjoy the view, boys, because most of you aren't going to see this again at the Welsh Rugby Union's expense.'

Nobody in the ground knew it would be another four long years before Scotland won another international, and during that time we suffered a total massacre at the hands of the Springboks, 44–0. One reporter was quoted as saying, 'We were lucky to get nothing.'

It isn't just when you are very young that international matches can have a huge impact on the choices you make in a rugby career or, amazingly, see men who help you make important decisions about your future.

I wasn't to miss an international at Murrayfield, apart from the New Zealand game in 1954 when I had 'flu, until I left university in 1968. I can remember the newspapers in 1954 before Scotland faced the mighty men from New Zealand saying, 'Scotland's best defence would be to dig trenches'. In the event I believe we only lost 3–0.

I was there when Scotland beat Wales in 1955 to finish our unwelcome run of seventeen consecutive Test defeats, when an unknown wing, Arthur Smith, scored one of the best individual tries ever seen at Murrayfield. He punted and fly-hacked the ball, regathering at least twice and making the Welsh full back, Arthur Edwards, look very foolish – although to be fair, Arthur Smith was so good he could do that to almost anyone. How little did I know that many years later both men would have a direct influence on choices I would make.

As an eighteen-year-old I remember the immediate aftermath of the 1963 Scotland vs Wales match at Murrayfield as the crowds were streaming away from the terracing opposite the west stand. Scotland had just lost 6–0 in possibly the most boring game of rugby I have ever seen. Clive Rowlands at scrum half for Wales kicked the ball into touch constantly, more than once just fifteen yards out from Scotland's line. In total there were 111 lineouts, and with no lifting they were a total shambles.

David Watkins, the Welsh fly-half, received only five passes in the entire game. I am certain this match was the tilting point for the 'Dispensation Law' forbidding kicking out on the full outside your own twenty-five that was to be brought in a few years later.

As a group of us were leaving, I became aware of two totally forlorn figures still leaning on a crush barrier halfway up the rapidly emptying east terrace, and to this day I remain convinced they were in tears. I knew them well by sight. One was Pringle Fisher, a dental student, as I was about to become, not yet capped, and the other was Jimmy Blake, never to be capped. They were Royal High School Former Pupils (FP), consistently the best rugby playing school in Scotland. Both were highly rated, and the newspapers had been encouraging the selectors to pick them for months. Pringle was capped against England at the end of the season, going on to captain Scotland, and Jimmy, the mercurial, exciting fly half selectors loved to leave out, was never capped. He was the Danny Cipriani of Scottish rugby, with huge ability but never the safe option.

This sight had a considerable effect on me because, whilst I loved my rugby, was sad when my team lost and sadder still when Scotland lost, I had never seen two grown men in tears over a result before. It made me realise how much the game could mean to people.

TWO

Murder Ball

Throughout those formative years between 1952, when I was eight years old, to 1963 when I was eighteen, my whole world of rugby took place at school. For any younger readers, you might find it strange that there was no such thing as mini rugby. From the very beginning there were scrums, lineouts and tackling, and fifteen-a-side teams. There was also no doubt that the boys chosen to play for the school understood what an honour it was to be picked. The proud history of Heriot's rugby was something we all grew up with and it was hammered home to us over and over again.

In our first year of rugby the better fifteen players were picked for the 5th Juniors, and I suppose that the two teams were selected from sixty or seventy boys who had no choice over their winter sporting activity. I had made my debut for the 6th Juniors but the next week I found myself playing centre for the 5th Juniors. I should add that the 6th Juniors were in fact the 36th and lowest side fielded by the school on many winter Saturday mornings.

There was rugby practice twice a week, either Tuesday and Thursday, or Monday and Wednesday, from September to March, and the days varied as you went up through the school.

Memories dim with age, but what I do remember was we used to get on the tramcar which was drawn up waiting in Lauriston Place outside the school. They transported us down to the school playing fields at Goldenacre at the far end of town where there were eight rugby pitches, and a huge grandstand opposite the 1st XV pitch.

I should add these pitches were filled most Saturday mornings at 9.30 and 10.30 and all our big rivals in Edinburgh – George Watson's, Daniel Stewart's and the Royal High School – had a similar number of pitches. Similarly, their pitches were full at the same time, so it is obvious there was a huge number of rugby teams in each of these schools.

At the other end of the playing field was the cricket pavilion where the junior school rugby was based. I remember it as a cold, damp, unwelcome place that smelt sour. Memories can be unreliable, but the smell was a cross between carbolic soap, linseed oil from the cricket, and an all-pervading smell of damp. We had to change there and were told in no uncertain terms that rugby kit consisted of ankle-high boots which had cork studs with three or four nails holding them in, blue school socks with garters to hold them up, blue shorts, but no underwear, certainly no gloves, and one of two jerseys. They were blue and white stripes and an all dark-blue jersey used to differentiate two sides, which we would change into for home matches if the stripes meant a colour clash.

For practice matches you knew how well you were doing by the jersey you were told to put on. The dreaded call would be when you were told to swop your striped jersey for a blue one, because that meant you had just been dropped.

It is the rugby practice matches that will remain with me for the rest of my life. Throughout my time at Heriot's from the 6th Junior XV to the 1st Senior XV, the practice never changed. There were no drills, no coaching, no tactics, just games.

The 6th Juniors played the 5th Juniors, and the 4ths played the 3rds in the year above, and the 2nds played the 1sts in the year above that. I assume there were games going on between the players who weren't considered good enough to represent the school, but every week one or two boys came up to our game, and one or two boys vanished to the lesser game, probably never to be heard of again.

These games were a matter of life or death to all of us madly keen small boys, and they continued throughout the ten years I was to play rugby at school. To be dropped after missing a tackle, failing to fall on the ball or dropping a pass seemed like the end of the world, and the shame of it stuck to you.

You had to play well for your team on the Saturday, outplay your opposite number in the practice match more than once, and then he had to play badly, to have a chance of being promoted. Come rain, hail or shine you went to the practice matches. To be fair there wasn't much choice.

The bellowed words, 'Try disallowed!' rang out loud and clear across the pitch, and I'm sure could be heard up to a mile away, and 'Penalty to Blues' are probably my first memory of practice matches at school.

A sharp blast of the whistle followed by, 'Smith you jumped up and down when More scored a try, that foolishness has cost your team three points. You must turn round and run back to your end of the pitch and get ready for the kick-off. Heriot's boys do not congratulate the try scorer, only footballers do that.' Said with a sneer as well!

So, we learned the hard way not to congratulate a try scorer. In fact, try scorers could almost have felt they were plague carriers such was the way their teammates turned their backs on them as they returned in triumph. Everyone just turned away and sprinted back to the half way line with not even a smile, lest the sound of the death knell whistle erupted in our young ears, and fear and trepidation as to the shame that could be inflicted on any one of us foolish enough to show any excitement or pleasure at all. Especially if we had been promised that the next try wins the game, and we could all go and have a bath.

This would shortly be followed by such a shrill blast on the whistle you fully expected uniformed police officers to appear and arrest the miscreant, but what we heard instead was one of these statements that struck fear into the heart of thirty little nine-year-olds.

'No try, Clark, you are wearing a vest under your jersey.'

'Penalty to Stripes. Brown, your socks are down, where are your garters, boy?'

'Penalty to Blues. Anderson, you are wearing gloves. Go back to the pavilion and take them off . . . Run don't walk, boy!'

'Alexander, you turned your back on the ball after I awarded that penalty. Another ten yards, Blues.'

You learned jolly quickly to back-pedal facing the ball when a penalty was awarded against your team. This went on week after week, month after month. Mr Donald M. Hastie and Mr Archie McIntyre ruled us with a rod of iron.

No matter how cold it was, all clothing accessories were forbidden, not even underpants were allowed, never mind a tracksuit. A second jersey under the first was almost a capital crime. Almost worst of all was the shrill cry of the whistle followed by, 'Stand still!' often followed by, 'Smith. What do you think you are doing? Stay where you are.'

At this point thirty little boys stood frozen to the spot, awaiting the announcement of their crime. We all knew where we should be, but overcome by laziness, cowardice or just plain inability, we were about to be shouted at, punished, or simply mocked. That's not quite true, because one or two of the more knowledgeable boys would less than subtly shuffle towards where they knew they should be, only to be yelled at, 'Stand still.'

Significantly, the boys who were shuffling, whose knowledge of the game was better than their peers, were the same group who used to turn up on a Saturday afternoon to watch Heriot's FP 1st XV, who were consistently one of the best club sides in Scotland in the 1950s and 60s.

I was one such boy, mostly because my father was so enthusiastic, and whilst the group of friends from school watched most of the games, we also kicked a ball around on one of the neighbouring pitches.

The lucky few, who oddly enough went on to become the stars of our schoolboy teams, names like Hogarth, More, Lewis, they always escaped the verbal lashes. I would like to say I was one such boy, but there was no chance of that. I always came in for an earful, perhaps, on reflection, because I had a cheeky face, and was prone to answering back, something that has sadly never left me.

The one thing this form of mental torture achieved was to very quickly make little boys know where they should be on the pitch. When you add the games of British Bulldogs and Murder Ball, there certainly was no health and safety here. I believe from the safe distance of over sixty-five years there are few better ways to find out who has ability, who has speed, who loves physical contact, and who simply doesn't want to be there in the first place.

Murder Ball was played by placing the ball on the halfway line and two equal teams had to lie down at either end of the pitch. The whistle would blow and both teams had to sprint for the ball, no kicking allowed, and the object was for one team to carry it through the posts at the other end for a score, then the whole thing would be repeated. There was method in this madness, because the quicker children became three-quarters, and the slower, often stronger boys became the forwards.

In British Bulldogs one or two players had to tackle called-out individuals and stop them running from the try line to the half way line. If a player was quick enough or could dodge well enough to get to the half way line then everyone else standing behind the try line could charge forward. Slowly but surely the number of tacklers increased and the runners became fewer. It quickly became quite obvious who could tackle, and who could run and beat a group of tacklers, and also the poor unfortunates who couldn't run or tackle. I know what you are thinking – they became full backs.

These games were also played in the school gym during PE lessons, which happened at least twice a week, and of course the gym staff liaised with the rugby teachers, and we soon were allocated positions.

At this stage I was one of the fastest in my age group, could catch the ball most of the time, and seemed to find passing quite easy, not that we did a lot of that, so found myself playing in the centre.

There was no 'tag' or 'mini rugby'. We were into contact, scrums, lineouts and fifteen-a-side from day one on a full pitch. No playing across the pitch between the twenty-five-yard line and the try line, and no coaches on the pitch, only the masters who refereed.

There were no non-slip rugby balls, no new balls or nearly new, just hand-me-downs. I remain convinced that the balls we played with when we were small were full-sized leather balls with a lace, that had started life as a new ball played with by the 1st XV. By the time we used them they had become slimy and heavy, which meant nobody was strong enough to land a conversion, especially with the eight-panelled South African balls. If the pitch was muddy, the ball became like a cake of soap, and if you adjusted it when you caught it then it was deemed a knock-on and a scrum had to take place.

If the pitches were frozen or snow-covered, a not infrequent occurrence in Edinburgh, then there was no question of getting home early. We still had to travel down to Goldenacre and run up and down and round the pitches to keep fit, and that was horrible.

To add insult to injury, after the practice was over we returned to a pavilion that had little or no hot water, just foot baths, no showers as I recall, and mud-coated floors. Our boots had nailed-on studs, so cuts and scratches were the order of the day, but amazing as it might sound, we loved it. Nevertheless, we came to look with envy at the boys in the senior school, who had passed their eleven plus exam, because they got to change in the new pavilion next to the 1st XV pitch, under the grandstand, which had huge hot tubs, and was definitely five-star accommodation by comparison.

The day ended with a half-mile walk to the tram, and then a thirty-minute tram journey from one end of Edinburgh to the other, followed by a six hundred-yard walk down my street in Morningside, all done with muddy knees, knowing a hot bath awaited. Eight or nine years old, often in the dark, and almost always on my own, twice a week it became a habit I would repeat throughout my time at school.

No fears, no nasty incidents, no dirty old men lurking in the shadows, no thoughts of them either. They simply didn't exist; we just looked forward to going home to high tea with our mums and dads. No cars on the road, or very few, and almost a total absence of cars parked at the side of the street.

I returned to my home in Nile Grove a few weeks ago, and there are now parking permits, and not an empty space to be seen. What a different world we live in today. There was no television to go home to, no computer games, no mobile phones, and whilst there was radio, it lacked anything we children wanted to listen to. This is what life was like in 1953, only eight years after the end of the Second World War. The year that sweet rationing ended, and dental decay returned with a vengeance.

So what did we do?

We went straight out into the street where friends from other schools had just returned from their sports fields. We played pick-up football, cricket, dodge ball, and a variety of other games using a tennis ball, more often than not under the street lights, and boy did we learn three things. The first was ball control, the second was climbing garden walls to fetch the many balls that didn't remain on the street, and the third was running away from a policeman on the beat, who knew exactly where we lived.

The other strange thing I remember clearly was the total lack of obesity. There are lots of different opinions about the shape of far too many of us today, and at the age of seventy-plus I must include myself. What I do know is this: there were absolutely no ready-cooked meals, in fact there were no supermarkets, no fast food outlets, and no snacking between meals. In my home, my mother was on her own all week because my father worked away, and she fed her three children extremely well, if predictably, because money was always in short supply. Monday was leftovers from the Sunday roast lamb, with the meat, potatoes and gravy all heated in a dish. Tuesday was very often ham from a ham hock which had been used to make soup along with lentils, onions and carrots. This soup would then be added to according to what was prepared on other days. The soup became thicker and thicker until you could stand a spoon up in it. We had no refrigerator at this stage, so the soup sat out on the cooker, and I can remember my mother removing the mould before boiling it again! Wednesday was often mutton stew, which was my absolute favourite. Again, mother was making soup and boiling the scrag-end of a neck of mutton, and then picking out the pearls of meat, which I can taste the sweetness of as I write. We would eat this with carrots and potatoes which had been boiling along with the meat. Mince and mashed potatoes and mashed turnip was another midweek favourite. Thursday was often cubed spam in a cheese sauce with hard-boiled eggs, and Friday was either fried fish and chips, or spam, egg and chips, although I do remember being allowed to stay up late as I got older and my father had come home for the weekend. He worked all week in Aberdeen so mother would cook his favourite things. This included mince with a poached egg on top, which was disgusting, or smoked haddock in milk, equally disgusting, or some rice dish which reminded me of vomit so to this day I will not eat risotto, but I, of course, being allowed up late had to pretend to like it.

We should all have hated Donald Hastie and Archie McIntyre, but at that time we were just little boys who were a bit scared and certainly in awe of them. Many of us over sixty years later still hold them in high reverence, for the standards they set us, standards that we wish were still maintained today.

At the end of season 1953/54, and after we had played our first few matches, we were ecstatic to realise that Mr McIntyre was no longer to be our rugby master, and he was to be replaced by a Mr Malcolm Hunter, a younger member of staff who we discovered still played occasionally for the club 1st XV.

Heriot's FP was one of the top clubs in Scotland along with many other similar old boys' teams, coupled with similar sides from Glasgow and town sides from the Borders, such as Melrose, Gala, Hawick and Langholm. They played each other throughout the season for an unofficial championship and Scotland teams were in the main selected from these clubs, with several players from England, nearly all of whom played for London Scottish.

It was, however, out of the frying pan and into the fire, because Malcolm was if anything even more scary than Mr McIntyre. He differently used sarcasm as a weapon, and withering scorn can be the hardest taskmaster of all, but he was to be involved in my rugby throughout the rest of my time at school, and without him I would never have gone on to have the level of success I had.

Malcolm had faith in me when I didn't have faith in myself and he liaised cleverly with my father to convince me where my best interests lay as a fifteen-year-old who thought he knew best.

The gratitude I have for these three men remains with me today, and it wasn't only the principles of what playing sporting rugby was all about, but more importantly the life principles they instilled in us. There was never any question of cheating. If you knew you had put a foot in touch (there were no touch judges), you said so, even if it meant not scoring the winning try. It was that kind of an upbringing.

The thing that was drummed into us incessantly was to learn how to tackle 'properly'. By properly it was the adage, 'the bigger they come the harder they fall'. There was tackling practice every week at Goldenacre, also in the gymnasium using rubber mats, where we were split into two groups standing in a line facing each other. The whistle would blow, and the person at the end of one line would run down the gap between the two lines of boys and the end person in the other line would have to tackle him. How we all hated that exercise, because it always seemed that you drew the biggest and fastest boy to tackle. All tackles had to be made below the hips as close to the knees as possible, heads had to be on the correct side, into the backside, and we were assured that tackling meant winning, and how wrong that proved to be.

It seemed to me, and most of my friends, that instead of 'the bigger they come the harder they fall' it should have read 'the bigger they come the harder they are to tackle and the more it hurts.'

Rather embarrassingly there is photographic evidence to suggest I never quite got the knack of getting my head behind the backside when tackling on my left shoulder, so it is little wonder I took a number of head knocks during my rugby career.

Looking back over sixty years I feel that the first experience of tackling should have been to tackle someone smaller than yourself, then when confidence had grown begin tackling bigger boys, but not when they were running flat out. Tackling practice frightened some boys, who never recovered, and whose tackling was always suspect right through school. Having been put through the tackling practice ordeal week in, week out it was quite demoralising to discover we had essentially been told fairy stories about how tackling won matches. This theory had one very serious drawback which we came to realise very quickly. Without going into too much detail at this point, the word 'passing' comes to mind.

One of the teams we played hadn't had all the tackling practice, instead they learned how to pass, and this side caused us a lot of heartache and grief.

THREE

The legend of Billy McCosh

There isn't a Herioter alive today who was born at the end of the war, who played rugby in the 5th Juniors, 3rd Juniors or 1st Juniors at the same time as I did, who won't remember Billy McCosh. In fact, I would go further than that, and say if you were born at that time, and were educated in Edinburgh and played rugby for the best team in your year, then Billy's name will be well remembered. I would be very surprised if he didn't cause carnage wherever he went.

Billy absolutely terrorised us for more than three seasons. He was a big lad for his age, quick, skilful and strong, and he went to the Royal High School. We seemed to play them every two weeks, and each time he just ran through us, like a hot knife through butter. Their ground was at Holyrood, right next to the palace at the bottom of the Royal Mile, and it was a journey made in fear because of that one boy.

I can still remember arriving at their ground and looking around nervously. No sign of Billy McCosh, thinking maybe he was sick, as a lot of us were in the early 1950s when measles, mumps and scarlet fever were commonplace. Your heart would stop racing, then, just as you were beginning to calm down, there he would come around the back of the pavilion, like some huge animal on the prowl, looking to destroy us. I can still feel the sense of dread.

The key for Royal High School was that their boys were all able to move the ball really well, so it could always be passed to Billy who would, inevitably, finish the move with a score. We couldn't pass nearly as well. We thought we could tackle – but no one could tackle Billy, so we were outplayed, and outclassed. Apart from the humiliation, what also annoyed us was they didn't tackle low below the knees like we had been taught to do. Instead they would grab jerseys, tackle round the neck, and we didn't feel that was fair, in fact we thought it was cheating and unsportsmanlike . . . but my goodness could they pass the ball well. Good running, passing and backing-up always beats good tackling. And then you add an ace to the pack like Billy McCosh and we just couldn't' live with them.

Our other tormentor in chief was Arthur Orr, a blond centre I can remember hating as a small boy, although to be fair as we got older, I began to develop a healthy respect for his ability. He had a degree of arrogance about the certainty that they would beat us every time we met, and I hated that too.

We realised quickly that we had to learn to pass the ball, or we would go on suffering defeat after defeat at the hands of the sides who could perform this straightforward task well. I wouldn't say it put us off playing but we just hated it, until one Saturday when I was in the 3rd Juniors, my second season of playing rugby, a boy called John McIntosh told us he had the answer. He said that if you threw a stick between someone's legs they would trip and fall, and that would soon stop Billy. We pointed out we didn't have any sticks, and anyway that wasn't allowed – and then he said he would be the stick.

What he did appeared to be suicidal, because he just dived

between Billy's legs, and made no attempt to tackle him, he just made Billy trip and fall using his body like the trip stick. I remember John crying with the pain, but he didn't cry as much as Billy, because we beat them 6–3. The myth was destroyed, and I think that was the first rugby match he had ever lost.

Royal High continued to get the better of us a lot of the time, and I'm sure Billy didn't lose many matches throughout his school career. He remains the outstanding schoolboy I played with or against and the Royal High School produced consistently the best and most skilful school teams we played against year on year, but the fear was no more. Billy remained a prodigious talent. It always meant a sleepless night every time Heriot's played the Royal High, and that was at least twice a season for the next six seasons.

The Royal High School teams we played against through the years had some really good individual players as well. Colin Telfer was an outstanding schoolboy who went on to play for Hawick and Scotland with great distinction. He was a year below us, and I can still remember talking to him before my last school game against the Royal High, and him telling the group of us that they had no chance because we were a 'team of old men'!

Names like Hugh Penman, who could so easily have played full back for Scotland had he not missed a few games due to illness, or David Fraser, a devastatingly quick fast bowler at cricket who once dismissed our first eleven, who were an extremely good side too, for about five runs. Bruce Laidlaw was a fine centre, who appeared in a Scottish trial, and toured Argentina with Scotland in 1968. In addition, they had Peter Orr, a very good flanker, who must have played 1st XV rugby from the age of fifteen. John Elvin was a talented scrum half, and David Pickering a hooker par excellence. The fact that all these years on I can remember so many of that Royal High group is a tribute to how good they were. Above all it was the confidence they had, their total self-belief.

I think it would be fair to say that we hated them at the time, but looking back they were well taught, with a lot of ability. Billy went on to captain the Scottish Schoolboys team that played English Schools on New Year's Day in 1962, and everyone thought he would win a Scottish cap. Sadly, I think knee injuries put paid to that, and when we met years later as grown men at London Scottish I couldn't believe how small he was! I suspect this giant of a nine-year-old was probably in an early adolescent growth spurt when we first met.

FOUR

You are too small to be a centre.
We want you to play full back

As a boy I won all my age group races in the school sports, and in fact the very first press cutting my father so lovingly kept was of the sports in June 1950, and a miniscule entry was the 80 yards under-6, winner I. Smith

As the years passed, I continued to win my races as can be seen from an excerpt from my father's notebook where, apart from 1953 when I had a broken leg, I won until 1957 when I stopped growing and finished second, until in 1958 when I finished fourth.

Significantly, when I was thirteen and in the second year in the senior school my height as seen from my father's records was just under five feet, when the average boy's height was five feet five inches. My sister, who is three years younger than me, was rapidly heading for five feet six and a half inches. It is little wonder I stopped winning any running races.

My parents were becoming very concerned at my lack of height. My father kept comprehensive records of all his three children's heights, running times, where we placed in our races, my sister's swimming times and, far more unfortunately, exam results.

My voice didn't break until I was fifteen which is why I remained so small, and embarrassed at my lack of body hair I used to wear swimming trunks in the showers after matches. I know my parents were very concerned about my growth because my father's brother Sid, who sadly died at Dunkirk, was so small he was known as the 'flying flea' at St Andrews University. I was told as a thirteen-year-old, 'You are too small to be a centre. We want you to play full back', and from the height record you can see why.

That was fine, though, because by then I was such a rugby fanatic, I knew all about the famous Herioters who had played full back for Scotland, and with the innocent enthusiasm of youth, I fancied my chances of following in their footsteps. Of course, if there were hinge moments in my rugby career, that was certainly one of the most important.

As a ten-year-old I had worshipped the ground that Ken Scotland walked on. He was at the top of the school and was the absolute star in the 1st XV. I always used to hang around after our 9.30 match to watch the school play on the 'big pitch'. He won match after match for them, scoring tries, kicking goals, and laying on tries for his centre Eddie McKeating who was to win his first cap on the same day as Ken. Eddie was the British junior sprint champion and tackled like no one I've ever seen since. The school 1st XV had a home and away fixture with Belvedere College Dublin and I watched the home fixture where Eddie cut down this huge, very handsome and very quick red-headed Irish centre. This was obviously something that didn't happen very often, and I later discovered his name was Tony O'Reilly, who was to become not only a hugely successful businessman but a box office success with the 1955 Lions in South Africa where, if my memory serves me right, as a seventeen-year-old he set a try-scoring record, and again as a Lion in New Zealand in 1959. Another player in that Belvedere team to achieve huge fame was none other than the late Terry Wogan.

Ken was picked for the Scottish Schools side and that became my ambition right there and then. The fact that he had colours for so many sports (he had two 'colours pockets' on his school blazer) meant that that also immediately became another ambition to emulate.

Hero worship is the only description I can give it, and I even used to touch his school blazer if he was in a crowd! I had photos of him taken on the Lions tour in 1959 all over my wall. Looking back, I am totally convinced that this desire to emulate his skill and success became a major reason I was able to play for Scotland.

Developing a skill at kicking a rugby ball was so important in those far off days as a full back. Rugby was a very different game compared to how it is played in 2019. Prior to the late sixties, full backs were very much the last line of defence, needing a very specific skill set of kicking, catching and tackling. Living in a terraced house with no real garden, just the street, I had to find somewhere to kick the rugby ball my parents had given me. About fifteen minutes' walk away, half that time if I ran, were school playing fields called Tipperlin that belonged to George Watson's College. I used to climb over the wall, and practise kicking until the groundsman appeared and chased me off. Sometimes a little Watson's boy would appear, and as with kids the world over we began to play kicking games, and he was very good.

We realised that we had played against each other in school matches, and I then discovered his name was Ian Robertson, now a very famous but sadly recently retired broadcaster. In fact since the loss of Bill McLaren, his dulcet tones on Radio 5 have made him very much the voice of rugby, and he will be much missed now he is no longer broadcasting. Our paths were to cross and coincide many times over the next fifteen years, and I owe him a huge debt of gratitude. Had he not appeared, I may have stopped going, and who knows what would have happened.

Also, his ability to give an inch-perfect pass was to give me my fleeting moments of fame in 1969 and 1970. Ian was very highly rated in Wales as a fly-half because back in the 1960s Watsonians used to tour there every Christmas and New Year playing against the likes of Cardiff, Swansea and Newport. Welsh crowds have always ranked amongst the most knowledgeable and critical in the world, so to have such a high opinion of a player meant a lot.

In 1956/57 season I was in the senior school, having scraped through the eleven plus. Teams in the first year of the senior school were given the prefix 'D'. In the second year 'C', and in the third year 'B'. In each year the teams numbered down from D1 to sometimes D8, and so on with the Bs and the Cs. Each of these three years could field up to eight teams on a Saturday.

I was playing for C1 in season 1957/58 when I was thirteen years old, playing full back and loving it, when disaster struck and shattered my confidence. This was the moment when I let a ball bounce behind our try line and then to compound the error tried to fly-hack it, missed it and the opposition scored.

In truth, I never totally recovered from that, and from that moment on I had a totally irrational fear that it would happen again.

I was to spend the rest of my time at school, and even after leaving school, trying to play somewhere else, anywhere but full back. Tragically at the time, but thankfully for my future, I just wasn't any good anywhere else.

The following academic year I was in the B1s and although I was suffering anxiety attacks, loss of appetite, even vomiting before matches, I was still a regular fixture in the side at full back. I found huge difficulty in catching anything, almost always wanting to let it bounce first. In hindsight this was ridiculous because I would spend hours kicking a ball with anyone that I could find, and never had any problem at all catching balls.

Stars were beginning to emerge, particularly Tony Hogarth, a flying winger, who was to go on to captain one of the most successful school 1st XVs ever, as well as becoming a top-class athlete.

In the third form I was really struggling in class. To be fair I was in love for the first time, with a girl called Christine Grossart. This despite the fact I was still in shorts because I wasn't tall enough to be allowed to wear long trousers, and my voice hadn't broken. I did almost no studying at all and my exam marks were so bad that I heard my parents discussing apprenticeships – in other words, taking me out of Heriot's.

There are several 'hinge moments' in everyone's life, and of course we don't recognise them until much later. By their very nature these are the times when decisions are made, and not necessarily by us, that decide the future direction of our lives, and they have far-reaching consequences.

Mum and Dad were both very academic; mother had been school dux at Madras College in St Andrews, and my father ended up with enough initials of his qualifications to fill one line of an envelope (W.A. Smith BSc Hons, B Com, FICE, FIEE, FIChE), so I had obviously not inherited their brains. My sister Aileen and brother Colin were both excelling academically, so I had become the major disappointment.

My father was sent for by the headmaster Mr W. McL. Dewar, and I will never forget that evening as long as I live. Essentially my parents' plan was very definitely that I should leave, and I was hiding around the corner of the stairs, fearing the worst, when my father returned home.

I remember quite clearly hearing him in astonished tones telling mother that 'Mr Dewar says Ian is very intelligent and he will have to retake the year but he will be put in the top class!'

This was a blessing in disguise, though it didn't feel like it at the time. As a youngster all you can think of is the fact that all your friends that you have been with for ten years are moving on. That meant that I had to try to make friends with a totally new group of boys who had their own established relationships. Having said that, the change definitely worked and surrounded by top academic children suddenly I began to gain top marks. To be fair it is a lot easier when you are studying the same course for the second time.

I owe a huge debt of gratitude to Mr Dewar. Not for the first or last time someone had faith in me, when I didn't have faith in myself. I have never forgotten him, or the amazing advice he gave me on my last day as a schoolboy. 'I'm going to give you the same advice I gave to Ken Scotland before he left. Study in the morning when your brain is fresh, then you can play all the rugby you want, and I'm sure you will go far.'

As I was once again to play third-form rugby, I was selected again for the B1 team at full back. I told the master in charge I wanted to be a centre as I was now about five feet four inches tall. He told me that was fine, but I would have to play in the B2 side. I really didn't care. I struck up a centre partnership with Ian Purdom, who was about my size. He tackled like a fiend, but had a bit of trouble with the ball in hand. I have very little memory of that season, except one of stress-free enjoyment, all of which was to change when I moved up into the fourth form in September 1960 where those who played for the B1 in the third year could expect to play 3rd XV rugby. This was also the first opportunity for exceptionally talented players like Tony Hogarth who went straight into 1sts and 2nds practice.

I was asked by the games master Malcolm Hunter if I wanted to play full back and said no. The response was that I was picked for the 4th XV. One week later, after the Saturday game where I thought I had played well enough, I was asked the same question, and gave the same answer, and found myself in the 5th XV, where I played fly-half and dropped a goal, the first in my career, and at that level they were as rare as hens' teeth. What is so funny to me is that I can remember it as if it were yesterday, down to where the pitch was, and the fact that the ball ended up on the road.

When asked the same question the following Monday, I still said I did not want to play full back and was promptly told, 'You will be playing in the 6th XV.' Here were the unwilling and the incompetent and my pride wouldn't let that happen, so I gave in, and on the Saturday found myself at full back for the 3rd XV.

I am now incredibly grateful to the master who masterminded this operation, although at the time I was angry and terrified again. The thought of having to catch, without letting the ball bounce, almost made me stop playing, except there was my pride backed up by the simple fact that this option wasn't available. My father would have gone berserk if that had been my decision, and I spent much of my youth desperate for his approval.

Within a short space of time the 1st XV went on their annual tour to Dublin to play Belvedere College. Disaster happened on this tour, and three of the 1st XV suddenly left the school, and I was summonsed to play full back for the 2nds in one of the weekly practice matches. At that time, the 1st XV full back was Ian Alexander. He and I had started Heriot's together as five-year olds, and we were friends. He had won his half colours, which meant he was an established first-team player with probably around seven appearances to his name. Half colours meant you could wear the school badge on your jersey, and you could feel you had a permanent position, but if Ian had a weakness it was his defence.

What happened at that practice match was another occasion that was to change my rugby life. Tony Hogarth, who was later to become an international high hurdler, so wasn't exactly a small man, broke free on three occasions, and each time I tackled him, which was a rare sight because up until then Tony had not been tackled too often such was his physique and speed.

Let me paint a picture of George Heriot's for those not from Edinburgh. The stunning main building, with a prominent clock tower built four hundred years ago, surrounds a quadrangle, is easily viewed from the esplanade of Edinburgh Castle. The quadrangle is entered from the Pend (a Scottish architectural term referring to a passageway that passes through a building to a courtyard, such as the quadrangle). The quad is bounded on the north and east by cloisters with pillars with rounded arches. The cloisters were used by the boys as a shelter in bad weather. At the end of the Pend is the beginning of the cloisters, and on entering the Pend you can immediately see the first pillar on the left-hand side.

On the pillar, slightly higher than eye level, was where the team list and awards of colours and half colours were posted. On a small sheet of white paper with the school crest at the top would be where you would expect to see the 1st XV team sheet. I must have passed that pillar dozens of times after the practice match, until finally my heart leapt, my pulse quickened and I walked as casually as I could to that little white sheet of paper pinned to the board on the pillar. At least being the full back, whose name came first, I didn't have to look far. There was my name on the team sheet, a moment I have never forgotten.

In a rugby-mad school, it didn't take long for the word to get around, and whilst it was amazing to have so many boys come up and say well done, it was all slightly tempered by Donald Hastie who called me into his room.

It wasn't so much a call as a note handed to me in a classroom, with the instruction, 'See me in my office at 12.40'. Here I was informed how lucky I was to be chosen, and what faith he was placing in me, against the advice of the other games masters. This was followed, if I remember rightly, by telling me not to let the ball bounce, and make sure I found touch. I don't remember the words 'good luck' or any real encouragement. It wasn't so much that he had confidence in me, more 'don't let us down', and this wasn't to be the last time I heard that sentiment.

When I got home I couldn't wait to tell my father who, whilst obviously delighted, also reminded me that I was now following in a great tradition of Heriot full backs, and I must always remember that.

In 1957, three years before the day I was picked for the 1st XV, I remember when Ken Scotland and Eddie McKeating got their first caps in Paris against France, and I had listened to the match on the radio in the kitchen. The broadcast seemed to be coming from another planet, fading in and out with more crackles and pops than Rice Krispies. Ken dropped a goal and kicked a penalty and Scotland won 6–3.

Looking back, I remember that this really was the defining moment when I knew that I desperately wanted to play for Scotland, but it also fuelled a desire to score all the points in a Scotland victory in my first international. I didn't ever tell anyone this, because it would have been thought of as one of the most stupid and unachievable dreams. Briefly the fear and terror were pushed into the background only to surface again and again, match after match.

Silly as it sounds now I used to play balloon rugby in my bedroom. The door at one end had a horizontal strut across the middle, and that was the posts and the bar. At the other end was my bed, and to the side of the bed was a small window, the base of which was about waist height, and that was the bar at the other end of the 'pitch'. I used to spend hours imagining myself in made-up international matches where I played all thirty players, but always managed to score the winning try or the winning conversion. They do say you have to dream something first for it ever to become a reality . . .

FIVE

Now do that with your right foot

Apart from the elation at being picked for the 1st XV, there was also that fear which was never to leave me. There are nerves, which are quite understandable, and everyone who plays competitive sport will suffer from them to a greater or lesser degree. What I suffered from was entirely related to playing full back, and the importance of the game had a part to play too.

Having said that, I desperately wanted to be a 1st XV player, and much more than that, much more, I wanted to play for Scotland. That meant I just had to overcome the way I felt because if I was going to make it then full back seemed to be my only option. If I was unable to overcome the nerves I had to somehow or other learn to live with them, and just find a way to cope.

I also developed another phobia and that was about the weather. I would wake in the morning, look out of the window and if it was windy it made my mental state even worse. This lasted throughout my rugby career, and I used to pray that we kicked into the wind in the first half, so I could at least enjoy the second half. I didn't mind the wet too much, although the balls we played with were leather, and certainly could be likened to a cake of soap when wet, and they were very heavy too.

In truth I loved it when it rained heavily with no wind, and the pitch was boggy and wet. My enjoyment was entirely based on the knowledge that there would be a lot of kicking, although my detractors always said it was because it slowed the others down to my pace! Lots of sportsmen have superstitions, and I now began to realise I had a routine that I had to follow. I always put my left boot on first and put the laces in as well. I must confess and am embarrassed to write it that my father always cleaned and polished my boots, and my mother washed the laces, so I always looked immaculate on matchdays. Donald Hastie would not allow players on to the pitch unless their kit was immaculate, and I was completely spoiled in that respect by my parents. To be fair, until I stopped playing serious rugby I would always clean and polish my boots before matches; I just never washed the laces!

The first time I experienced what it was like to play with a new or newish ball was in the 1st XV and it was unbelievable to be able to kick it some distance because it was light in comparison to the balls I had played with.

Rugby in the fifties and sixites was totally different to the rugby played today, because the full back was very much regarded as the last line of defence, and not as an attacker. He needed to have good hands, ideally be able to kick with both feet, and to tackle anything and everything. Positional sense was regarded as a necessary virtue, because wings were wings, and not auxiliary full backs. In fact, wingers in many cases were picked for their speed and not for their rugby ability, or their good hands, or their tackling either!

The amount of kicking was prodigious, thus the need for a full back to be able to catch, kick cleanly and find touch, because there was no limit on where you could put the ball directly into touch.

What this meant was, and this certainly applied from the time I made my school 1st XV debut in 1960 until I stopped playing full back in 1972, that you could guarantee one of the first things the opposing fly half would do was to send up a high ball just to see if you could catch it. If you dropped it or knocked it on then this would be repeated at regular intervals throughout the match.

Worse than that was the early kick you had to run for to catch before it bounced. I found that very hard initially, and it was the thought of knocking the ball on that really worried me all the time. My father, who was my best supporter, was also my biggest critic, and to come home after playing what I thought was very well, he would always include the words, 'It's a pity you missed a tackle. You took your eye off the ball for the knock-on, and the time you missed touch could have been crucial.'

Sometimes I would dread going home.

Anyway, I made my father promise not to come to my debut for the 1st XV on the big pitch at Goldenacre.

This was the moment I had dreamed of, coming out of the tunnel as part of a team, and not just drifting on to the pitch as we had done for years. Also, you would be in the 1st XV dressing room with its own bath and showers, and not shared with anyone. You entered the back of the stand in the middle at Goldenacre, turned left, and went past the groundsman's office where the terrifying Alec Gillies, head groundsman, ruled the roost. You could see him standing behind his counter distributing old wet heavy leather balls to small boys without so much as a smile on his face, but plenty of threatening comments about what would happen if the ball wasn't returned.

Alec saw and helped generations of Heriot's boys in his own way and with his own style of encouragement! In other words, he scared us all rigid. I do remember quite clearly how pleased I was the day he used my name, whereas before I had to tell him what it was. The feeling that somehow I had arrived made me feel six inches taller.

On through a door, and into the changing area, and the 1st XV went in the first door on the left. Each player had a locker, and I found out very quickly that lockers were 'owned' by established players. I think the captain had the first locker on the left inside the door, and as the newcomer I made the mistake of using a senior player's locker, albeit briefly as I was put firmly in my place, my bag hitting the floor at some speed!

The best bit was running out under the large grandstand on to the 1st XV pitch. I'll never forget that feeling as you went down a slight slope between railings, and there were always people leaning over wishing you luck. There was a slight upslope, then a step on to the grass and then on to the pitch.

The main pitch at Goldenacre was sacred turf and coming out to play for the 1st XV would be the first time you had ever stepped foot on it. To put even a toe on the pitch as a boy was to invite certain death from Alec Gillies, or what felt like it by the roasting you were given. We even had to warm up on a back pitch. That made a special moment even more special, and to be playing on a pitch with a grandstand which seemed huge. All school rugby up to that point had been played on back pitches in front of a few proud parents on the touchline. The 1st XV, on the other hand, could expect a hundred or more spectators, and even the possibility of the press being in attendance, so there might be a report in the evening sports papers.

I think I played well enough in my first game against Robert Gordon's College from Aberdeen, I didn't make any mistakes and I had my first experience of a newspaper report, which said both full backs had been safe and sound.

My father came to watch and, in an attempt to stay hidden, stood at the end of the large grandstand, so that when the game came to his end he could step back into the shadows.

That worked until I had to go off the pitch to fetch a ball and I saw him flattened against the side of the stand! His attempt at anonymity had failed, and strangely enough I never worried again about my father watching.

Having survived my debut, I was anxious to play the next match, and I managed to keep my place in front of Ian Alexander until the end of the season and was awarded my half colours. Some fifty years later I was to discover that Ian Alexander had been the only 1st XV half colour to lose his place and never get it back. Once again Donald Hastie and Malcolm Hunter must have seen something in me that I didn't see in myself.

By Heriot's lofty standards, season 1960/61 was an unmitigated disaster. Captained by Bryan Chapman, the side lost a lot more than it won, which was something that hadn't happened to me before, so I wasn't sad to see the end of that 1st XV season.

As a youngster I began to play a lot of tennis. In the summer term when you reached the third form if you didn't want to play cricket or do athletics you could play tennis. Cricket and I were never going to be friends, and it was utterly frustrating to be too small to win any athletic events.

While I was never going to set the tennis world on fire, I was twice a semi-finalist in the East of Scotland under-18 singles and was fortunate enough to have some fantastic doubles partners. I partnered John Clifton in the East of Scotland doubles which we won, and he dominated Scottish junior and senior tennis in the early sixties and went on to play in the Davis Cup for Great Britain. I think I got to play with him because of my rugby!

My school doubles partner was a small boy, David Abbott, who was a far better tennis player than I could ever have hoped to be, but he was asthmatic and quite frail, although he went on to be the Scottish Junior champion.

Heriot's had entered the Clark Cup for Schools, a tournament which was to take place on the hard courts at Wimbledon, and David and I were the second team. To everyone's surprise we reached the semi-final where we played RGS High Wycombe and were soundly thrashed. Our tennis master, Mr Barr, had asked the legendary Dan Maskell to run the rule over us, and afterwards he told me that Dan Maskell's opinion was, 'Tell Ian Smith to stick to rugby.'

We also met the legendary Fred Perry who gave each of us a tennis shirt, telling me I looked like a boy with a sense of humour, and when I got home, discovered it was a girl's shirt!

I was to have three seasons in the school 1st XV, and lucky enough to be picked for the Edinburgh Schools for two years, then, in my third season, to be picked for the Scottish Schools. That was a once-a-year fixture, played on New Year's Day, and to my sadness the fixture in 1963 was cancelled due to snow and frost.

Two things happened that were then to have a lasting impact on my rugby career. The first was when Mr Donald Hastie came across one afternoon at Goldenacre and asked if I would give Ken Scotland some kicking practice. I'm sure you can imagine how I felt, both nervous and elated in equal measure. We stood on opposite sides of the pitch on the twenty-five-yard line and kicked back and forth. It quickly became obvious that my right-footed kicking was pathetic, my left-foot screw kick didn't work too well, and I fumbled a lot of balls. The plus side was the encouragement I got from Ken, and just to be in the company of a Lion, and my hero as well, was quite overwhelming. But it showed how hard I needed to work on my kicking and my catching.

The second was at an Edinburgh Schools training session when I was standing at the corner flag screw-kicking the ball so it went between the posts. It was my party trick, and I could do it about one in three times. I was feeling quite pleased with myself when this voice behind me said, 'Now do that with your right foot.'

As I was almost exclusively left-footed I turned round with a cheeky grin on my face to see Mr Mitchell, the famous master in charge of rugby at the Royal High School, standing there. I said something along the lines of, 'Don't be silly, my right foot is for standing on.'

His reply was to the effect that I could be good enough to play for Scotland but not until I learned to kick with my right foot, because the selectors would know and judge me on that basis.

That was a real hinge moment in my life because that was the very first time anyone in authority had ever said anything like that – about maybe playing for Scotland. That statement about my right foot came back to haunt me, and throughout my rugby career it was continually mentioned in one form or another. I was even described once in *The Scotsman* newspaper as being 'as one-footed as Long John Silver'.

Mr Mitchell's comment galvanised me to try very hard to kick right-footed. It took a good six years from that point before I could trust myself to do it in a match, but I eventually mastered it.

With experience I discovered that being left-footed at full back was actually an advantage. Most fly halves were right-footed and tended to kick while running to their right; if they kicked towards the touchline and I fielded it, then I was able to comfortably return the kick down the right touchline – a much easier skill as a left-footer.

When I first played for the 1st XV I used to compare myself to my opposite number, but after two or three years I realised my real opponent wasn't the other team's full back but their fly half.

Any time I've coached a young full back, one of the first things I've suggested is to note whether the stand off is right- or left-footed. A lot is spoken about being two-footed but very few are. The position a full back takes up is very much determined by the fly half's kicking foot. I realise this will not apply at the top levels in twenty-first century rugby where the wingers have most of the skills of a full back, but as this account relates to my own playing days it was very relevant to me.

As a Heriot's schoolboy playing for the 1st XV, coming out on to the pitch at Goldenacre to a full grandstand and with most of the touchlines crowded was an unbelievable experience which will live with me forever. The first time I experienced this was playing our local rivals the Edinburgh Academy on a Wednesday afternoon.

I can clearly remember as a youngster being let out of school early to scramble on to one of about twenty tramcars lined up in Lauriston Place that took us up Goldenacre for the Academy match. I also can vividly picture what seemed like hordes of Academy boys in their school uniform and school caps descending on the ground. The atmosphere was electric enough then, but to actually come out on to the pitch to play in front of a packed ground as a 1st XV player was one of the highlights of my life then and remains so now.

As far as I can remember, the Academy were unbeaten when we played them in 1961 under the captaincy of Tony Hogarth. We had lost just once, so it really was a big fixture for a school match, and fortunately the sun shone with no wind.

That Academy match was really the first time I was subjected to a barrage of up-and-unders from a fly half – in this instance, Jeremy Sands, a multi-talented sportsman who went on to play cricket for Scotland. It was also the first really good press report I ever received, which was thrilling. They had two massive forwards in George Menzies and the future Scotland and British & Irish Lions legend, Roger Arniel, with whom I was to play for Scotland eight years later. The match ended in a hard-fought draw. Naturally, my father kept the newspaper report, which said: 'In the latter capacity I.S.G. Smith fielded all the Academy's tactical kicks with calm confidence and usually returned with interest. He could, however, put in a bit of work on his right foot.'

There was the right foot issue rearing its ugly head already!

Our next fixture was against Merchiston Castle, who were a school I had never beaten – but in 1961, following our draw with the Edinburgh Academy, we felt we were in with a great chance.

This was a Saturday fixture, and whilst we had a good level of support, Merchiston, as a boarding school, bussed all their boys to Goldenacre and easily outnumbered the home-team's crowd. In the early 1960s boys, by and large, cheered good play no matter which side was responsible. Once again the atmosphere was incredible and we recorded our first win at 1st XV level against Merchiston for ten years, and my first ever. It was possibly our best achievement in what was an outstanding season. Their full back, Robin Gray, was the most accomplished full back I had ever seen, and this was a stage in my own development when I was beginning to wonder what my rugby future might be like – and I never thought I would or could be as good as him.

It's funny the things that stick in the mind. I remember that some of their players, including Robin Gray, wore fingerless gloves during the match. Imitation is said to be the sincerest form of flattery, and so it proved here. I went home after the match and got my mother to cut the fingers of some old school gloves so that I could play like Robin. But it was hopeless. When it was muddy the mud stuck to them; when it was icy (which was frequently, as Edinburgh winters in the early 60s were often very cold and icy), the wool collected little lumps of ice; quite honestly, they were more trouble than they were worth.

I remember both of these matches, plus the defeat by the Royal High School earlier in the season, as some of the most exciting games I have ever been involved in, so when I came to check on the scores when writing this book, I was somewhat surprised.

Heriot's 0 – Royal High School 5
Heriot's 0 – The Edinburgh Academy 0
Heriot's 5 – Merchiston Castle 0

And then finally at the end of the season:

Royal High School 0 – Heriot's 0

When you compare these scores with match results in 2019 you would question how on earth they could have been exciting. To fully understand I suppose you have to appreciate that to play 1st XV rugby at Heriot's or any other major Edinburgh school was a massive thing at the time and, of course, rugby was such a different game then. On the flip side, high-scoring games today can actually be quite boring and not necessarily as exciting as they sound. Meanwhile, 3–0 can be real nail-biting stuff for players and supporters alike.

One of the biggest influences during my teenage years was the Scottish Schoolboys Club. They ran camps in Perthshire twice a year, the first at Easter at Dalguise near Dunkeld, the second in the summer at The Falls of Bruar, near Blair Atholl. I camped twice every year without fail from 1957 until 1968.

Sport played a huge part at these camps and it was said that since the early 1920s no Scotland rugby team had taken the field without at least one former camper in their ranks – including the likes of Eric Liddell, Ken Scotland, Dougie Morgan, Gordon and Peter Brown, Finlay Calder, and many more besides.

At SSC camp, hours and hours would be spent kicking rugby balls to and fro, almost always in gym shoes, sometimes in bare feet. At Easter, the campsite was on a hill, and to be at the bottom of the steep hill having balls raining out of the sky, when you didn't see them kicked in the first place as you ran avoiding tree stumps, tent guy ropes and other campers going about their business, proved great training for a full back.

The only warning you might get was a cry of 'catch this!' and a ball would suddenly appear high in the sky from a kicker standing a good thirty feet up the hill.

I didn't know it at the time, but appreciate it now, that all the hours spent doing something I loved was preparation for an opportunity that would arise in the future.

It was at one of these camps that I was taught the rudiments of screw-kicking, that spiralling punt, which if done properly can fly for miles and is a beautiful sight to behold. It saddens me how rarely we see it used now in the first-class game. I have been told repeatedly that the way the ball is kicked today is more accurate because there is less room for error. There is certainly less distance kicked, although occasionally you are lucky enough to see a world-class fly half kick an inch-perfect screw kick diagonal which skids into touch close to the corner flag. Men like Ronan O'Gara, Andrew Mehrtens, Johnny Wilkinson and Dan Carter, all of whom had the ability to make a rugby ball 'talk', were just such a joy to watch.

Over the years I worked very hard on my kicking out of the hand – or punting the ball – and eventually was able to hit the perfect screw kick nine times out of ten. My technique was honed – my controlling hand was always over the ball and I slammed it on to the outside edge of my boot so it didn't wobble and the contact was virtually identical every time. This did two things: firstly, I could guarantee huge distance, regularly hitting sixty yards, and that with a leather ball unlike the modern ball; secondly, slamming the ball down dramatically reduced the chances of a kick being charged down because it sped everything up. When I watch kicks from fly halves being charged down it is almost always because the ball is almost thrown up by the hand and not forced down, so everything takes fractionally longer.

I also rarely see the screw kick used as an up-and-under, and it is such a lethal attacking weapon. Often players kick the ball into the air when they have time to set themselves. The spin which causes the ball to move sideways mostly comes out at the end of the spiral, so if it is done vertically it makes life close to impossible for the receiver on the ground. If you add in the fact that if the receiver sets himself to jump, the ball isn't going to land where he thinks it will. I'm sorry to have diverted the reader, but in my youth a full back was expected to be able to screw-kick, and from the time I was first taught until I stopped playing I devoted hours and hours to that art.

In December 1961 I was fortunate enough to be picked for the Edinburgh Schools XV to play Glasgow and the North & Midlands. Tony Hogarth and I were the only Herioters, which was somewhat of a surprise as our school team was considered the best in the country by the press.

On my wall at home I have a photograph of the Edinburgh Schools XV captained by the fearsome Erle Mitchell, who I was to get to know and work closely with at Edinburgh University, and I still have the programme for the match against the Glasgow Schools.

In that Edinburgh side were the future Scotland half backs, Gordon Connell, who also played for the Lions, and Ian Robertson; Bruce Laidlaw, who toured Argentina with Scotland and played against the Pumas (although no caps were awarded for Tests against Argentina in those days); a future Scotland hooker in Bob Clark; the future Scotland second row, Erle Mitchell; and myself.

In addition, the Edinburgh Schools XV had four top-class coaches involved – Mr Mitchell, who coached some extremely successful Royal High School sides, Donald Scott, who coached at Watson's and was a former international himself, Alex Harper, who was the rugby master at Trinity Academy, and our own Donald Hastie.

When I look back at the North & Midlands team we faced that season, one name stands out – that of Scotland and Lions centre Chris Rea, more of whom later.

These games were my first taste of representative rugby and more than a little nerve-racking, but were essentially three scratch sides muddling through. No matter, playing in that team gave me a sense of enormous pride.

Moving into my last year at school I looked forward to a successful final season in the 1st XV, but much to everyone's disappointment, the 1962/63 season was drastically shortened by snow and ice and we played no rugby at all from December until March.

Despite this, the tail-end of the season was very enjoyable. I was picked again for the Edinburgh Schools and received my best press report ever when we beat the Edinburgh Academy in what was always regarded as one of the top school fixtures of the year.

'Outstanding in the Heriot's defence was their experienced full back ISG Smith,' wrote *The Scotsman*. 'Apart from fielding and kicking immaculately, Smith averted at least two certain scores, once when he put in a lifeline tackle, and once when he turned and beat JN Sands in a long race for a loose ball.'

Moving on to my last game for the school 1st XV, my father by this time stood out on the touchline. I had never scored a try in my three seasons of first-team rugby until that day, and when I was running down the pitch to score, my father took off after me along the touchline, and pulled a hamstring and had to be helped into the pavilion! Thus my final match as a schoolboy culminated in my only try for the 1st XV, which was a lovely way to end my time there.

Earlier that term I had begun to apply for university and, initially, I was very keen to go to St Andrews because that was where my father had studied – but I received an unconditional offer from Edinburgh University and decided to go there instead. Little did I know how big an impact that decision would have on my rugby career.

SIX

You have to be a lot quicker
if this is going to work

I left school as a nineteen-year-old in 1963, and in the September, whilst waiting for the university term to begin (where I was to study dentistry), I turned out for Heriot's FP. I was picked at fly-half for the 2A XV – in other words, the '2nd-2nds'. This sounds better than the thirds, which of course it was! The chances of 1st XV rugby as a full back were non-existent at the time with Colin Blaikie, an internationalist established there and Ronnie Scotland, Ken Scotland's younger brother, his understudy in the seconds – which made me secretly relieved. It also gave me the excuse to play in another position, but after kicking a penalty early in the season for the 2A XV, I felt something funny and hot inside my knee. A visit to the doctor told me I had a piece of floating cartilage, and it needed complete rest . . . so that was season 1963/64 gone.

The next season I began playing again at fly-half for Heriot's 2nd-2nds and in September we went down to at Walkerburn in the Borders for a game. Halfway through the match, I got kicked right in the middle of my left forearm and had to leave the field. Luckily, I discovered that the local doctor was a Herioter, so I was taken there in the middle of a Saturday afternoon where he saw me in his home. What chance of that happening today? It would have been a four- or five-hour wait in A&E, but there he was in his slippers, smoking a pipe. He took one look at my arm and uttered the fateful words, having discovered I was a dental student, 'That's the end of your rugby career, laddie.'

He said I had fractured one bone in my forearm, possibly two, and as a dentist you couldn't afford to take the risk of not being able to work. His words took me right back to my family dentist, a lovely man called Douglas Millar, who played rugby for Watsonians, and the number of cancelled appointments I had with him because he had damaged hands and arms. I'd recently passed my driving test so had driven to the ground, with my father's stern advice about not having an accident ringing in my ears – little did either of us realise the accident wasn't to involve the car!

I drove myself to hospital one-handed with my left arm in a sling, changing gear and steering with my right hand. Now A&E in the Royal Infirmary in Edinburgh on a Saturday evening was a sight to behold, and I ended up on a bench with six or seven other sportsmen, all still in our sports kit, waiting on our X-ray results.

I had to wait for hours for the X-rays to be developed and then dry. Eventually a doctor came along the line, and some guys were sent to the plaster room, but thankfully, and to my amazement, I was sent to be strapped up, and told it was bad bruising and I'd be okay to play again in a couple of weeks.

It was about this time that three of the senior players at Goldenacre – Bob Tollervey, the late Jimmy Simpson, and Ian Palmer – took me to one side and advised me that my best course of action would be to throw my lot in with the university side. There was little immediate future at Goldenacre with their roster of players and they felt that I was too good to wait around in hope of filling dead men's shoes. They told me that the university had a first-class fixture list and I should be able to make the team.

Whilst it was good to hear that these three wise old birds rated me, I was first and foremost a Herioter. I wanted to be a Heriot's FP full back playing for Scotland, so in that sense it was a crushing disappointment. This might seem a strange remark as I have not long since declared I had lost all confidence as a full back, but I knew in my heart of hearts that was where my future lay.

They were of course being totally realistic and I had watched Colin Blaikie winning matches with individual brilliance often enough to know that I had little or no chance of displacing him.

I turned up for the university trial matches in October 1964, having missed the first in October the previous year. I didn't put in a great performance, mostly because a chap named Ray Newton was selected at fly-half, who had played for English Schools at full back, and he kicked the ball higher and further than anyone I had ever seen, putting me in all sorts of trouble.

Unsurprisingly I found myself in what is known as the XXX Club. Edinburgh had strange names for their teams because under the XXX Club could be found the Vikings, the Vandals, and, finally, the Vagabonds. All five teams played at least once a week.

There was no such thing as a coach, but Erle Mitchell's father George ran rugby with an iron rod, and unless his approval was obtained, promotion to the 1st XV was out of the question. After a couple of weeks, I managed to play well enough to earn his grudging approval and found myself listed to make my debut against a team called the Co-optimists.

The Co-optimists are kind of a Scottish Barbarians, in that they are an invitation club only. For aspiring players, it was always a goal to be asked, as most players based in Scotland at that time who were to go on to play for Scotland had played for them at least once.

Sadly today with professional rugby, the Co-optimists don't choose, or cannot choose, top-class players. In my time, current internationals would play in matches to open clubhouses, floodlights, and memorial matches, that kind of thing. The Co-ops selections always had a heady mix of experienced internationalists, potential internationalists, district players, and highly thought of club stalwarts.

I don't have the best of memories about my debut. One strange thing that I do recall was that David Rollo, the legendary Scotland and Lions prop, who had been a fixture in the side forever, announced that day he was retiring. To a twenty-year-old that seemed incredible – how could anyone give up playing rugby?

The second (and very painful) memory was being involved in trying to tackle Ronnie Glasgow, who was an international wing-forward, at the same time as someone else came in from the other side, trapping my left arm, which I had injured at the start of the season while still playing for the 2nd-2nds. The agony was instant, but this was my debut, there were no substitutes, so there was no question of leaving the pitch. I didn't look for any kind of contact after that but that evening, even ten pints of beer down, the pain didn't lessen.

A visit to casualty at the Royal Infirmary followed and the doctor who brought my X-ray in said, 'When did you break your arm before, because it has fractured through callus?'

When he got his hands on my previous X-ray from the few weeks before it showed that I *had* broken my arm at Walkerburn but my X-rays had been mixed up with some other poor chap also called Smith, who must have been walking around Edinburgh with his unbroken arm in plaster all that time. It seems very funny now, but at the time I was heartbroken. I now found myself with my first two seasons out of school unable to play because of injury and was left feeling that perhaps my ambition to play for Scotland was never going to happen.

The following season, 1965/66, was the time I finally began to get a toehold at full back for the university 1st XV. Every week David Boyle, the captain of the side, made it clear that my tenure would be short if I didn't excel. He couldn't make up his mind about whether to play Ray Newton, the ex-England Schools full back at fly-half or full back. His other option was to bring in Billy Wood, who could play fly-half, full back or wing.

This made me practise my catching and kicking even more intensely to eliminate errors and increase my self-confidence. Training took place at the university seconds' pitch at Canal Field, which rather sadly is now a housing estate. There were lights, although hardly floodlights in the modern sense, almost the equivalent of street lamps, and the fact that the ball could be kicked up into the dark, with very little time to see it, improved my catching no end. Only seeing it late was not dissimilar to my days as a boy at the Schoolboys camp, standing at the bottom of the hill only seeing the ball for a short time.

Training, by and large, was all fitness – just running, sit-ups, press-ups, and then followed by touch rugby, which was the only real time the ball was used. It made for a trying season, which I only just survived, but was awarded my 'half blue', or a 'green' as it was known in Edinburgh.

As a team our biggest difficulty, particularly against club and Border teams, was that we didn't get enough ball because of the relative immaturity of a student pack of forwards.

We had the basis of a very good team for the next season, but I was by no means certain to be in it as both Ray Newton and Billy Wood were very much still around. Ray was by now a full blue and turning into a top-class fly half, so I hoped him transferring to full back wasn't going to happen.

Billy, like myself, had a half blue, and there was always a question about who would arrive as a fresher straight from school with high-class credentials. This was both the good and the bad in university rugby. You could be a half blue, think you were established, yet lose your place to a new undergraduate who was a top-class player.

It was at the end of season 1965/66 that I heard the university rugby club needed a new honorary secretary, and many sources told me that 'the secretary is always in the 1sts.'

Without any hesitation I applied, but had I known exactly what was involved I might not have been so keen! I have written several times about hinge moments. Well if ever there was one, this was it. Literally it was a decision that was to change my life forever.

To give you an idea of what was involved, the rugby teams, all five of them, were posted in a passageway behind the McEwan Hall and opposite the Anatomy Building at the university. This was very close to the Student Union which, I may add, was a male preserve at that time. This happened twice a week throughout the two winter terms so, as you will see, it wasn't a small job.

The Dental School was about five minutes away at a trot, but it could take longer because the chances of meeting teammates and friends in that part of the university were very high. The five teams for a Wednesday were posted side by side on a Monday, and on a Thursday for a Saturday.

Effectively, medical students Erle Mitchell, the captain, and Richard Rea, his vice-captain in season 66/67 picked the 1st XV and thus the XXX Club, but as secretary I picked the Vikings, Vandals and Vagabonds.

It is important to realise that there were no mobile phones, students by and large lived in flats with no phones and only those of us who lived at home had a contact number. Putting the team sheets up was the easy bit, and players were expected to 'cross on' showing they had seen their name and the instructions about where to go and when to get there. Those players who were unavailable put a line through their name – and then the fun began.

If a player called off from the 1sts, I had to get hold of the captain, move someone up from the XXX Club and do the same for the Vikings, Vandals and Vagabonds. Call-offs didn't just happen once, but sometimes ten times a day, so every player had to check the board constantly to see if they had been moved up.

The Vagabonds had a wonderful captain, a rotund Welsh medical student called Dai Williams, who had an infectious and permanent smile, with an incredible ability to conjure a side out of nowhere. He was a regular fixture in the Union Beer Bar, as were most other medical students. The regular announcements on the loudspeaker asking for anyone who wanted a game of rugby to come to the entrance hall mostly came from Dai. That he managed it most weeks was a triumph and totally down to his personality, although I got the credit!

Vagabonds rugby was everything that Michael Green's *The Art of Coarse Rugby* epitomised. As an aside, I believe competitive leagues and the need for an insane number of substitutes who might travel for two hours and only get a few minutes on the pitch has been the death knell of what was a vital part of the game's heart and soul.

To return to the team board, by Wednesday lunchtime, as you might imagine, it looked like modern art gone mad, and my level of fitness was partly due to the number of times I raced to the board to change and move players before rushing back to a clinic. I have to add that my mother was magnificent, because my telephone number was one of the few readily available, and I would come home from a lecture on a Tuesday or Friday, or the library at eight o'clock in the evening, to find a list of up to ten call-offs waiting. There were times she even told players which side they would be in, and in some respects, she became an additional selector.

My one reason for doing the job soon became a reality as I established myself as the 1st XV full back. We had an excellent side emerging at the time, helped enormously by the fact that a large proportion of the team were medical, dental and veterinary students, meaning that we were all at university for at least five years, which gave us some added maturity, which, especially in the forwards, was a big help. It also gave the side a chance to really meld as a team, and the results became amazing.

Edinburgh University in season 1965/66, captained by David Boyle, were not a bad side at all, and it formed the basis of the hugely successful teams in the following two seasons. At that time our future stars were still too young and lightweight to cope with the age and experience of club packs of forwards. We would get pushed about in the set piece, and generally forced back up the pitch by the older and more mature opposition forwards. We then relied entirely on our fly half, Ray Newton, to send our opponents back seventy or eighty yards with his booming boot. He kicked a rugby ball further than anyone I have ever seen, and that includes the modern players. There was little refined technique to his punt – he just hit it, and it would fly seventy yards down the pitch, without spinning at all. I could screw-kick most of the time; Ray didn't, in his case it was just huge power and timing.

Ray had three other magical qualities, the first of which involved the railway line at Craiglockhart, which was deep in a cutting behind the stand. When we were getting tired, Ray would simply kick the ball over the pavilion into touch and down on to the railway line. Three kicks like that and all the match balls were used up, and we got a rest whilst someone made the three- or four-hundred-yard journey down to the local station to get on to the line to pick up the balls, and then retrace his steps. In addition, the ball-finder would take his time because he knew that for Ray to lose three balls like that meant we definitely needed a rest!

The second thing was his goal-kicking, which was prodigious. When I see modern players placing the ball on a tee on their own ten-metre line and kicking goals it instantly reminds me of Ray. The huge difference is the balls in the sixties were leather, heavier and there were no kicking tees, just the mud scraped up into a mound. Ray used to point the ball miles away from the post, hit it with a dull thud and it would fly like a scud missile seeking its target, wobbling up and down, never reaching the height of the posts, but with an accuracy that was unerring and invaluable. The number of matches Ray won for us with his boot was huge. Why the England selectors never came calling has always remained a mystery to me.

Ray's third quality was with the ball in hand, and this almost more than any other was to dramatically change the way that Edinburgh University were to play their matches.

By 1966/67 we had developed a very decent pack of forwards headed by the formidable Erle Mitchell, who took no prisoners. I'd lived in fear of him since school, as far back as the 1st Juniors, when as an eleven-year-old he played for Melville College. He had captained the Edinburgh Schools side I played in and had a deserved reputation as a man who would punch if there was a need for it, and sometimes when there wasn't. You would fall on a ball at his feet and risk life and limb, as his rucking technique would be a credit to an All Black.

When he became captain of the university XV in season 1966/67, he built on David Boyle's hard work and leadership and brought his own brand of confidence-building. After scraping a win against a team we should have lost to, his famous one-liner was, 'They had nothing positive to offer.'

Erle was a brilliant two-handed lineout jumper, especially at the front of the lineout. You have to bear in mind that there was no lifting in those days. Lineouts were a war zone, but he could guarantee to pinch a good portion of the opposition throw-in.

Erle and our pack of forwards just loved Ray Newton. Week in, week out there would come a point in the match when an opposing pack's heads would go down when Ray had just sent them back fifty yards yet again with another booming touch-finder. For a pack to work hard gaining forty-fifty-sixty yards and then be sent back from whence they came by a kick must have been devastating, especially when it kept on happening.

The problem, however, was that while we potentially had the cutting edge outside the scrum to score enough points to offset the constant pressure on our young lightweight pack, we definitely lacked the how-to to execute it. In other words, we were doing exactly the same things as the opposition but with less ball, and that was no way to win matches.

We certainly had the talent, but we just couldn't get enough good ball over an eighty-minute match. The teams we played had talent as well, because it mustn't be forgotten we were playing most if not all of the top clubs in Scotland at that time, but with more ball to play with they were almost always going to have the beating of us.

What it did mean was that in season 1965/66 we closed the gap on many of the top sides without really being able to win. Even Cambridge and Oxford universities beat us regularly and we inevitably lost to the likes of Gala, Hawick and Heriot's.

There seemed to be no real solution to this, not that we as students lost much sleep over it, we were having too much fun. Unexpectedly, however, there was an answer just over the horizon the following season and none of us could have believed how simple and successful it would be, or what the long-term impact was to be either.

To explain to anyone brought up watching or playing the modern game it is difficult to believe that it wasn't until 1969, almost a hundred years after the first rugby international, that the Australian Dispensation Law was enacted which didn't allow kicking into touch on the full outside the twenty-five (now twenty-two). The immediate effect of this was to open up the game and bring more tries.

If you are still relatively young you won't remember there was a time when full backs were primarily defenders, who were expected to be able to catch everything that was kicked at them, and also to be able to kick with both feet. Tackling anyone who broke through was also considered essential for a good full back. That was all there was to it unless you were a Ken Scotland who could beat anyone on a sixpence and who scored wonderful individualistic tries during his career.

The words 'back three' were not in existence, and now fifty years on the professional game bears very little resemblance to the rugby we used to play, with a multitude of tries scored in almost every game. In fact, rugby is now seeing basketball scores, which is not something the old-stagers totally approve of. If you ever get the opportunity to watch an old movie of a rugby international from the 1950s and 60s and compare it to the modern game you will be staggered at the difference.

Have you ever asked yourself how this modern way of playing rugby ever began, or whose brilliant idea it was? Be certain of this, someone somewhere was the genius whose ideas changed the role of the full back forever.

I was privileged to have been involved, although not as an instigator, but a very fortunate participant when set-piece moves involving the full back first appeared. To be totally honest, I can't remember the moment it happened. There was no blinding flash of light, no sudden realisation that we were on to a winner, or that what was about to happen would have a serious impact on the way rugby was played, and not just locally either. Looking back, it is hard to believe that a bunch of students who loved their rugby, but also believed in having a good time, could come up with some simple moves that would enable our side, often outgunned in the pack, to win matches week after week that we would have lost previously.

In fairness it wasn't a collective brainwave, in other words we as a team definitely didn't suddenly come up with new ideas. They very definitely belonged to a diminutive Irish medical student by the name of Harry Rea and date back to the early part of the 1966/67 season. Harry was small in stature, but big in heart, did not bear fools gladly and was a perfectionist in every way. If my fading memory serves me right, he arrived back at university in late 1966 from Belfast with some crazy ideas about running the ball and using the full back with predetermined moves to create an overlap.

A quality centre who should have won more Irish caps than he did, Harry should have been given more credit for the way that back play developed from the day he put his ideas into practice. Sadly, as happens with many ideas-men, he has never received the credit he was due. In fact, outside the small Edinburgh University group he was involved with, the rugby world at large remains in ignorance of his inventive genius.

What Harry proposed were some set-piece back-division moves, using the full back, which seem very simple by today's standards, but were unheard of then, and not one club in Scotland were using them or anything similar. It wasn't new for full backs to come into the line, that had happened for years, but not the way that Harry planned. More important than that, teams had no counter to it, so from the end of season 1966/67 and particularly in season 1967/68 we ran riot against some of the best club sides in both Scotland and in England.

It involved the fly half, two centres, and the full back, and I had the great good fortune to hold the full back position at that time – although I realised very quickly that I was going to be doing a lot of running.

There were three basic moves. The first was the simple 'miss one' where the fly-half missed out the inside centre, passed the ball straight to the outside centre and then to me. The second was 'miss two' where the pass went from the inside centre, missing out the outside centre, once again to me between the outside centre and the wing.

The third was simply a dummy scissors between the fly half and inside centre, followed by a pass to the outside centre and once again to me coming in at full back. I think there was a fourth, which involved a double dummy scissors between the fly half and the two centres with the pass coming to me, but I can't be sure.

Now all of this was fine, but for two things, which made life a little tricky bearing in mind my apparent lack of pace. Firstly, I wasn't allowed to stand in the three-quarter line, I had to stand behind the fly half, or between the fly half and the centre, and deep enough to make it appear that I was ready for the opposition to kick. Prior to that, and all too often today, the full back is standing in the line so there is no thrust to the move.

Secondly, I was expected to be running faster than the outside centre, effectively accelerating into the gap between the outside centre and the wing. This acceleration would take me through the first line of defence and up to the full back whereupon I would draw the full back and pass it to the wing. The key to the whole thing was that I had to be running faster than everyone from five yards behind the outside centre, and the pass had to be flat. I realised early on that I could be running as fast as I could for over forty yards before I was in a position to receive a pass.

When we first began to try it out, on a Sunday morning after a Saturday evening's beer drinking, it was very hard work. Sunday morning sessions became part of our lives, though, because the training lights at Canal Field were woefully inadequate and not everyone could attend evening training sessions as many of our medical students were now working in hospital wards, and potentially two-thirds of the side faced this difficulty.

Very quickly I realised that with my basic lack of speed I had to start running very early – before the scrum half had his hands on the ball when we won a lineout or when the ball reached the feet of the number eight at a scrum. This meant total trust in the accuracy of the scrum half, fly half and centres' handling, because if a ball was dropped then I would have difficulty recovering my position. That, in fact, is an understatement. What needs to be remembered is that wings were not auxiliary full backs back then and our quickest winger Ted Osborne was far from renowned for his handling.

Secondly, the passing had to be flat and absolutely on the money, for nobody was spin-passing in 1966 except possibly Gareth Edwards in Wales.

Thirdly, the timing had to be perfect otherwise the centres would be caught in possession or I would get into position too early or too late. I certainly got the thick end of Harry's tongue every Sunday for what seemed like forever. I used to hear a loud angry voice, 'You have to be a lot quicker if this is going to work.' If I heard it once I heard it a hundred times. He was a perfectionist, thank goodness, because the Sunday morning sessions were the place that made me good enough to get into a position to challenge for selection for Scotland. Without the rudeness, encouragement and criticism from Harry, it could never have happened. Needless to say, I will be forever in his debt, not that I would ever tell him.

The great thing was it worked, and it proved that hard work and practice does make perfect. Edinburgh University began to be able to beat teams who had thrashed us for years, simply by being able to take the one or two good balls, we were able to create and take tries. We didn't need to achieve parity in the forwards, we just needed one or two opportunities.

There were a number of reasons the university side was so successful at this time. In my opinion, we had players in all of the key positions mentioned previously who could have, and of course some did, play at international level. There really wasn't another team in Scotland who had anything like as much natural ability at that time, so it shouldn't have been a shock when we led the unofficial championship from the start to almost the finish for two years.

We trained most Sunday mornings, Tuesday and Thursday evenings, and often played Wednesdays and Saturdays. The most remarkable thing of all was the fact that we were almost injury free. Either we did something right, the game of rugby was less dangerous then, or there is something very wrong with the game in the twenty-first century.

In addition, we dared to be different and we had the talent to be different. We couldn't play traditional rugby because we simply didn't have the weaponry up front, but what we lacked in bulk we made up for in speed and some great rugby intelligence outside the scrum.

Never forget that the dispensation kicking law wasn't active in the UK in season 1967/68, so when we started our back moves with the full back in the line, nobody had a clue how to counter it. Add to this we mostly carried the moves out from what is now first phase, or from a ball against the head, and did it from almost anywhere on the pitch. Plus we had the enormous boot of Ray Newton who could destroy a team's morale by driving them back time and again with monstrous kicking.

One of the most rewarding things in the two seasons of 1966/67 and 1967/68 was how we increased our following at Craiglockhart. The ground had a funny little wooden open-air stand, and in the beginning of my time in the 1st XV in 1965/66, the stand would be half full, with a scattering of spectators around the pitch. At the end of 1967/68, the spectators would be two or three deep around the ground because we played such attractive rugby.

SEVEN

I told him, 'If you do that again, I'm going to kick your fucking head in'

What luck that we had three of our best players involved in the critical part of the moves. In fairness I must include Arthur Espley, another medical student at scrum half to make that four, because if I leave him out he'll never forgive me. Arthur fought a spinal problem for much of his time at university, but was a class act, and another Irishman who should have gone further in the game. I watched him outplay every scrum half we played against, including several internationalists, and one Lion.

The main architect of our success was having a fly half who could pass twenty yards off either hand, and the ball would remain vertical as well, making it easy to catch. Just remember that in the 1960s the spin pass was something scrum halves did, no one in the three quarters would have dreamt of doing it, and forwards generally speaking didn't want the ball in their hands anyway!

You see not only could Ray pass the ball accurately over long distances, but he also understood the importance of the flat pass, so we were always stretching to get there.

When we won a lineout ball or scrum ball anywhere on the pitch we were good enough to call a three-quarter move. In the latter part of season 1966/67 and also in 1967/68 no one had a clue what was going on. I used to find myself in acres of space, and we could create tries from out of nowhere.

All I know is that I would never have played for Scotland if Ray and his two partners in crime in the centre hadn't been at Edinburgh University at this time, or if David Boyle had played him at full back!

Harry Rea was unlucky to get so few caps for Ireland, because he was our thinker. Unfussy, unglamorous, very brave, and very precise, he was also sometimes anonymous, not because he played less than well, but because he did the unfussy, unspectacular work so well. Harry was unfortunate because he formed a good Irish centre combination with Barry Bresnihan, with Mike Gibson at fly half. Then the Irish selectors then decided to go with Barry McGann at fly half and Gibson in the centre.

In the university team, we had John Frame in the centre, who went on to have a very distinguished international career, and his timing of a pass made for many, many tries, some of which I was fortunate to score, but many more for our contrasting wingers, Stuart Briggs, Ted Osborn, Billy Wood and Blair Morgan. Stuart and Billy were both skilful footballers with superb hands while Ted, possibly the quickest thing I have ever seen on a rugby pitch, had to have the ball virtually placed in his hands to make sure he caught it. When he did, he simply disappeared. He was that quick. It came as no surprise when I discovered some years later that he ended up with a double blue at Oxford for athletics and rugby. Blair Morgan came into the side in 1967/68 and was high on the try-scoring list as well.

John was a huge man in every sense of the word, totally reliable, never flustered, and had an immaculate sense of timing. Playing with him so often at university was the reason, without any doubt, why I was able to score two tries for Scotland – because I just knew the exact second I would get the scoring pass. He never went for the dummy or the try himself, he simply created it, totally unselfish in everything he did.

What a privilege to have played with such a good set of three-quarters; and to give you an idea of the quality, we had a centre called Neil MacMillan, who was good enough to play representative rugby for North and Midlands, a South African called Keith Kinsella, who had played for Natal, and Ray Megson, a gifted fly half who went on to become a top international referee, and all three spent most of their time in the XXX Club.

A side can only win matches if it wins the ball, and as a back even I have to admit that. Erle Mitchell was the godfather of the side and, as I have already alluded to, not above a bit of violence. In fact, he was the most violent man I ever played with or against, and he almost never got caught.

In November 1967, Erle won his first cap for Scotland against the touring All Blacks, as did John Frame, and an old friend and opponent Bob Keddie from George Watson's. For his first cap, Erle found himself marking the legendary, and sadly late Colin Meads in the lineout. Readers of the history of rugby will remember this as the match where Meads was sent off for kicking David Chisholm at a ruck, but that isn't the point of this tale.

In those far-off days after the International Dinner, which took place for the players, they would often appear in the Edinburgh University Student Union, and sure enough in came Erle arm-in-arm with Colin Meads, both in their dinner jackets, ties askew and definitely not sober.

I asked Erle how it went, and he said that at the first lineout he jumped for the ball, only to be punched in the face by Meads and sent sprawling. I was surprised that he seemed to have taken this literally on the chin without any retaliation. The second lineout came with the same result.

Incredulously I asked Erle, 'What did you do about that?'

Erle said, 'I told him, "If you do that again, I'm going to kick your fucking head in."'

'You said that to the most violent man in world rugby?'

'Yes, but I said it very quietly.'

Erle was to win only two more caps, because sadly he really wasn't quite big enough to be an international lock, and he always reckoned he only got his third cap because, as a doctor, he could push back the piles of one of the selectors!

There is no doubt in my mind that the success enjoyed by the university side at this time was totally down to the positive mental attitude Erle gave us. He could also eat a mean curry, and his favourite Saturday evening ending was always a 'phaal', which is the hottest of all curries, and he would sit, bright red in the face, while discussing the next match with his secretary and his vice-captain, Richard Rea.

Richard was much, much more than just the famous Harry Rea's elder brother. Without a doubt he was another player who could easily have graced an Irish international jersey. He could prop and play in the back row with equal success. He began his career in the university side as a flanker, then moved to the front row. Richard could play almost anywhere and much later in our rugby careers I played fly half to his scrum half!

He was regarded in the mid sixties as being too small for an international prop, and sadly by the time the Lions tour of '71 to New Zealand had come and gone it was too late for him. On that tour Canterbury famously tried to punch the Lions frontline players out of the first Test match that was to follow a week later. As a result of that match the Lions lost their two frontline props – Sandy Carmichael who had numerous facial fractures, and Ray McLaughlin with a broken hand. This meant bringing in the diminutive Sean Lynch and Ian 'Mighty Mouse' McLauchlan to the Test team. McLauchlan scored the winning try by charging down a kick, and the two small props got under their counterparts in the set scrums, and the era of the small prop began. Sadly, that was too late for Richard, who by that time was a qualified doctor serving in the Royal Army Medical Corps.

Richard became captain after Erle, and it was under his benign dictatorship that Edinburgh University began to play some unbelievable rugby. We knew we could score tries no matter where we were on the pitch because the back moves were so well practiced.

Memories fade with the years, but there were several other outstanding contributors to the success in the university pack. If I only name three or four that is because they were in my opinion the standout players, the exceptional players. The rest of the forwards were just bloody good!

The first, and in no particular order, was another Irishman from Campbell College Belfast, Patrick Irwin. He was an absolute natural openside wing forward but trying to get him to commit to rugby was very difficult. He'd rather be skiing or womanising, two other things he was extremely good at. On a rugby field he had an explosive energy, and a fantastic engine that could run all day. I'll never forget my one game for Scottish Universities when he snaffled two tries in the first few minutes as only a great wing forward could do.

The second most influential forward in the group was undoubtedly David Boyle. Good-looking and a very smooth ex-public schoolboy, he was also a classy number eight who seemed to know instinctively where the ball was going to be next. He had superb hands and a great rugby brain, but was possibly a little too likeable, and not hard enough to play at the higher level his ability justified. David seemed fairly set against me when he was captain in 1965/66, but he made me work harder on my fitness, catching and kicking, and he really laid the foundations for the huge success we had as a team in the following two years.

Thirdly we had Victor Bean at hooker, who was a veterinary student, and appeared on the radar when the Veterinary College, commonly known in Edinburgh as the Dick Vet, came close to beating the university side in what would have been a major upset. Our hooker, David Dummer, who was about to graduate and had been a fantastic servant to the rugby club, needed replacing and Victor came along and more than filled the bill.

I had a slight degree of social difficulty with Victor after my engagement to Maureen suddenly ended in fairly dramatic fashion. It was after a Cambridge University match where I had spent a long period of time in the bar and she threw her engagement ring at me and stormed off the dance floor, leaving me to scramble around on the floor hunting for what was a family heirloom. She had a fairly brief fling with Victor afterwards, plus one or two other members of the rugby club, which kind of shut me out socially!

When we got married eventually in 1969, a telegram was read out at the wedding which said: 'From Victor Bean, don't worry, Maureen, I've burnt the letters'! My response was exactly what Victor would have sought!

It would be less than fair to leave Rob Flockhart out. A back row forward whose bravery could not be questioned, borne out by the fact he ended up as president of the Scottish Rugby Union!

At the end of 1966/67 I was feeling pretty happy. I felt I had played well, had some good press, and most important of all there had been no catastrophes!

With the season over as far as the university was concerned, in the April I was chosen to play for an Edinburgh 'B' side. Having failed to get selected by Scottish Universities, this was certainly recognition from the Edinburgh selectors, and that was huge encouragement.

I was playing for Edinburgh B side against Edinburgh and District Juniors, when I suffered another kick to my left arm, my elbow this time. The big difference here was that I had to trudge back to a distant pavilion unaccompanied, in fact ignored by the district selectors, try to shower and change and dress using one arm.

Eventually I managed to get to the car, and with the gear stick needing a left arm, had to drive and change gear with my right hand. As I drove back into Edinburgh I saw my father out shopping, and pulled over to tell him what had happened. Big mistake. He panicked, and I thought he was about to have a heart attack, so I had to drive him home before proceeding to the A&E. The X-ray this time showed that the tip of my elbow, a bone called the olecranon process, had cracked halfway. The orthopaedic consultant was called, as it seemed to be an unusual fracture. Perhaps because I was a dental student, and supposed to be able to understand these things, he showed me the X-ray. I could see the crack through the bone, which he said was stable, and he put my arm in a plaster up to the shoulder, and only slightly bent. This was not the usual plaster that you hold across your chest in a sling. He said that would put too much pressure on the elbow, and the muscles could pull the olecranon off. Famous last words, as a couple of hours later I was at Maureen's flat having supper. In case the chronology has confused you, this was before she broke off the engagement! As was her habit, she expected me, the wounded warrior, to help dry the dishes. As I was doing so, I flexed my fingers on the draining board and there was an almighty bang within the plaster. This was immediately followed by a very sharp pain, and I knew that exactly what the surgeon had been trying to avoid had happened.

Back to casualty, this time on a bus, as I couldn't drive because of the pain, and we didn't have enough money for a taxi. I had to read my own X-ray, which showed the elbow completely detached, so I was booked into the consultant's clinic in the morning.

The consultant's clinic was full of medical students, including a good number of the university rugby team, and I was greeted by a few boos and a lot of laughs, until the consultant explained what had occurred, and what he planned to do about it. The new injury had bled into the elbow joint and that blood needed to be drained off or I would get what is called a haemarthrosis. This would have left me with a stiff elbow joint forever, and definitely put an end to my rugby career. The plan, he explained, was to numb the elbow and then insert a hollow needle to withdraw the blood. The injections were jolly sore, and then he informed his class, 'Now that I've given Mr Smith an injection it won't hurt.'

The only thing was I knew that it wasn't numb – and I'm certain he knew as well! Eventually I persuaded him to let two of my rugby friends hold me still while he proceeded. The pain was unbelievable. What was almost worse was trying to keep silent to preserve what reputation I had for bravery.

The next day I went to the operating theatre and a large screw was inserted into my elbow, where it remains fifty years later. A squash ball became my friend as I was told to continually squeeze it to help get full movement back. The consultant personally supervised my recovery, which all these years later makes me think he felt responsible for the angle he put my arm in the plaster in the first place.

I was able to play in the first match of the next season, which was about five months away. This was in September against Jedforest, but the limited movement in my elbow meant I could no longer put both arms in the air to catch a high ball. Now I had to turn slightly to the left, which was no bad thing, because it limited a knock-on as I was sideways on if I dropped anything. I was fine running left and catching, but not as comfortable running right as my left arm was slow to come across. Being left-handed didn't help either, but I was still able to play, and defied the consultant's advice.

Strangely enough, despite two arm fractures, I was still able to play three seasons for the university and only missed the very last match due to exams, which is amazing.

EIGHT

What do you mean you dropped fourteen balls?

My family used to holiday in St Andrews every August and, as a student, I used to train at the Madras College grounds with the former pupils' team.

In the summer of 1967, post-injury and just after I had won my blue, I did a lot of kicking practice with their full back, Colin McLeod. He had played representative rugby for North and Midlands and I had a huge respect for him. I owe him a big debt of gratitude for the success that was to come my way. Sadly, as has happened so often in my life, he passed away far too young and I never had the chance to tell him.

Colin asked me how many times I had dropped high balls the previous season, and my proud response was fourteen or fifteen out of about thirty matches. Expecting him to praise me, I was staggered by his outrage. 'What do you mean you dropped fourteen balls? That isn't nearly good enough. You should have been able to tell me you hadn't dropped any!'

He informed me that there were knowledgeable people who felt I could play for Scotland, but not if I dropped that many balls in a season.

The next season I was to drop eight balls in thirty-four matches, seven of which came about on one horrendous afternoon at Mansfield Park when we lost the club championship.

When someone you respect says that, it quickens the pulse, and does make you try harder.

As a boy learning, albeit unwillingly, to be a full back, there were skills that were paramount, and to have any chance of playing at a higher level you were expected to have faultless hands as a priority.

Great hands were therefore a requirement fifty years ago – the only real problem was the fact that match balls were leather and had all the characteristics of a bar of wet soap when it was wet and muddy, not an infrequent occurrence in a Scottish winter.

The second attribute was courage. Full backs could expect to be bombarded with high kicks early in a game, and the ability to stand your ground, make a catch, dig your heel in and call for a mark was very important indeed. It isn't funny to stand under your posts five minutes into a game knowing that this was the acid test. A good fly half could literally drop an up-and-under on a sixpence, and often you were all too aware of how close you were to the posts. The realisation that a dropped ball meant a conceded try, and the prospect of an afternoon fielding similar mortars was not a happy one. Add to this the inevitability that players would arrive at the same time as the ball, and while they couldn't, in theory anyway, hit you early, they would certainly smash into you as you caught the ball. That thought was small comfort indeed.

To digress, I just don't like the modern game where players can compete for the ball in the air. Firstly I think it is dangerous, secondly I feel it has in some ways reduced the impact of the high ball. Additionally, a player can call for a mark while running simply by putting his hand in the air after he has caught it. It is far more courageous to have to be standing still waiting for the ball and the opposition to arrive.

Finally, jumping in competition with an opponent gives the catcher an excuse if he fails to catch the ball. There should be no excuses and you need a huge amount of courage and skill to stand your ground and take the inevitable impact.

In the early sixties the university side really weren't very good at all. By 1968 we had come a long way. To try to give you some idea of the road we travelled, I will begin at Bedford RFC when we played them at Goldington Road in 1965. At that time, it was very definitely boys against men, and we lost comfortably.

This was hardly a surprise considering they had the England captain, David Perry, and included the English legend, Budge Rogers, plus a pair of international centres in Geoff Frankcom and Danny Hearn. In fact, with more than a couple of trialists as well, it would have been a miracle not to have lost, bearing in mind that Bedford were then, and are still now, in the top sixteen or seventeen clubs in England.

I have never forgotten that weekend, as the local paper insinuated I was suspect under the high ball, which rather ruined my breakfast. Then shortly before kick-off we were sitting in the changing room with the sun shining through the glass door. I, as usual, was trembling in my boots, when the light was blotted out by this man mountain, who turned out to be the fearsome David Perry. I'm still not sure all these years later why I should have been so scared of a man just because he was the England captain. On reflection, it was a massive deal for this Edinburgh lad to be playing against a top English club. I can still remember as a small boy watching in awe as Heriot's FP hosted the famous Harlequins, who seemed like gods – little knowing they would one day be just another club side I was to play against.

On that day Bedford were mature men and we were young callow students, although significantly the hard core of the university side were to stay together over the next three seasons.

We returned in 1967 as part of our university-funded tours to England, which took place every season, and we alternated between Oxford University and Cambridge University one year, and Bedford and United Hospitals the other year. The funding we got from the university for these jaunts was incredible. When Richard Rea was captain, and I was once again secretary, we went to Bedford not long after Danny Hearn had broken his neck and was sadly paralysed.

England were due to play the All Blacks at Twickenham, so our match kicked off in the morning. The previous evening was the Bedford Rugby Ball, to which we had all been invited, so naturally we went along assuming the Bedford side would be there as well.

It was daylight when I got back to the hotel, and the game was due to kick off some three or four hours later. It then transpired that not one of their 1st XV had been at the ball, which struck us as being somewhat unfair. Conned and not for the first time!

So, 20–0 wasn't a bad result considering the previous night, and that was in our favour!

I still regard that as one of the best wins of my whole career, bearing in mind that Bedford were probably one of the top ten clubs in England at the time. If we ever needed proof about how far we had travelled as a team then that was it.

What followed afterwards should perhaps have a veil drawn over it, however. It's all very well to drink into the evening after a match starting at three in the afternoon, but when the match finishes at 12.30, and you are on tour, and there is a television set to watch the international, it is only natural that some serious beer consumption takes place.

We ended up in a boat club on the river that evening, where they were having a dance. By the side of the dance floor was a sack and in that sack was a white powder which contained whatever was used to make the dance floor easier to slide on. Someone suggested it might be fun to whirl the bag around, so that's exactly what I did, only one end was open, and everyone in the room was covered in the powder. I left in a hurry, pursued by several ghost-like figures, and managed to keep ahead of them as I ran for the Bridge Hotel where we were staying – this involved running across the parapet of the bridge over the river, which I did without a second thought. I have been back to the scene of the crime since and realise all too well I was one step away from serious injury, even death.

I ran into the hotel and, leaning over the empty porter's desk, swiped every room key I could lay my hand on, including my own, and locked myself in the bedroom.

I was woken at about 2.30 a.m. by Richard Rea asking for the keys, and he told me later that the main compensation for the inconvenience of not being able to go to bed was seeing the evidence that I had been somewhat unwell, of which, of course, I have no recollection.

Back in Scotland, we enjoyed another great win when we played Gala, one of the top Border clubs, despite most of our side having come back on an overnight train from Cardiff on the Friday after playing for Scottish Universities. I think that we had around about twelve players involved, and they must have been exhausted.

Anyway, with ten minutes to go, Gala led 10–0, following which we scored four superb three-quarter tries straight from the Harry Rea playbook, and they simply had no answer, leaving us 18–10 winners.

Another memorable match was going to the Greenyards to play Melrose on a Wednesday. This was a fixture that was totally new to the team, because of the way rugby was organised in Scotland at that time. It is important to understand that there were no official leagues in those far-off days, but there was an 'unofficial championship' and you needed a certain number of fixtures against other clubs to qualify.

Edinburgh University did not have enough fixtures in season 1966/67, but we had a hundred per cent record, so I was tasked by Erle Mitchell to get more fixtures, and Melrose – one of the strongest clubs in Scotland – were one of the fixtures I managed to arrange. They were more than happy to accommodate us because no one in the Borders wanted to see a bunch of cheeky young students win the title, and at that stage it looked very much as if we were going to do just that.

The Greenyards has to be one of the most attractive grounds in world rugby, surrounded by hills and rolling countryside and the whole place just breathes history. Of course, it is where Ned Haigh invented the seven-a-side game, and throughout my childhood my father took me every year to see my heroes play in the sevens tournament there. I used to crawl my way to the front of the crowd and lie on the ground watching the likes of Ken Scotland and Tony O'Reilly weave their magic, and then try to get their autographs. All this time my father and his best friend, Peter Aitken, would steadily drink their way through the day and we'd all eat cold bacon and egg rolls made by my mother. The trip home took hours as my drivers stopped at every pub and with no breathalyser to worry about, people drank and drove with impunity.

Anyway, I digress; we went to play Melrose in 1967, and drew with them, which was pretty impressive, even if the game wasn't of the best. The next year, in 1968, we shocked them by winning. Afterwards they showed us a lot of respect, some of it grudging. This was not only because we'd won, but because we'd committed to the fixture when we had a lot to lose. These two matches were my first encounters with Jim Telfer, who was an absolute legend to me. He had been a Lion in 1966 and I was quite terrified by the man, and remained so, even when I played under his captaincy for Scotland.

Memorable matches don't always have to end in victory, and indeed playing against Hawick as a student never had a happy ending, although on one occasion it was very funny.

In 1966 we had gone to Mansfield Park and the weather was absolutely foul. Not only was the pitch very muddy but it began to snow, then that became a blizzard, and it was freezing. We had to face the wind and the snow in the first half and I think we had held Hawick to a credible 9–3 at half-time.

I remember Harry Rea with blue fingers, in tears from the cold, as we stood outside in the freezing conditions and sucked oranges – no retreat to hot tea and sandwiches in the changing room in those days! I remember David Boyle refusing the referee's offer to call off the match because he felt with the wind and the blizzard we were in with a good chance. That was until George Stevenson, the Scotland centre, scored under our posts early in the second half and David took up the referee's offer to call the game off.

As we trooped off the pitch towards the changing room I stopped to chat to my parents, and as I left to go into the pavilion apparently my mother asked my father who it was they'd been talking to! Looking at myself in the mirror I didn't recognise the mud-encrusted figure peering back either.

Edinburgh University played Heriot's in season 1966/67 at Goldenacre, and we beat them 12–11 when we led the Championship and they were lying in second place. For me to play at Goldenacre against a number of my old school teammates was a very odd feeling. It was made even more so by being confronted by my best friend Tony Hogarth flying towards the line at the very end of the game, and being able to tackle him, especially when the match hung in the balance.

When they came to Craiglockhart the next year, we beat them 26–0, which for Heriot's at that time was unheard of. A lot of Herioters were now very angry with me, and when we went down to Goldenacre for a drink that evening, I was told in no uncertain terms to get a member to sign me in as a guest, with the comment, 'You're no Herioter.'

I was very upset by this because several unkind comments came from people I had known all my life, even older men who had encouraged me to go in the first place when they thought Edinburgh University were fairly useless.

Before concluding this sorry tale, I have to mention the destruction of the university side by Hawick in a game we had to win, to become champions. We lost 31–0, I dropped eight balls, and in one game unravelled all the veneer of confidence I had built up over the previous two or three seasons. Apart from anything else, it was the second season running that Edinburgh University had fallen at the final hurdle so to speak, but on this occasion I felt personally responsible having played so badly.

I was to be carded as a reserve for British Universities, and played one final game for Edinburgh B on the anniversary of breaking my arm, scoring two tries, which was some compensation after the broken arm the previous year, and I was picked and played twice for the Co-Optimists.

I was then informally approached by Gala who were recruiting John Frame to partner Jock Turner in the centre. They had Drew Gill on the wing, and I thought Russell at full back was as good as I was, probably, and without my hang-ups. Edinburgh Wanderers made encouraging noises as well, but to be honest after the Hawick debacle I just wanted to get as far away from rugby as possible. I had really had enough of the pressure not only of playing rugby, but also running five rugby teams for two seasons alongside the burden of degree exams. I also wanted to get out of the country after graduating and decided to join the Royal Army Dental Corps.

As a postscript to the season 1967/68 I came upon another cutting lovingly collected by my father and dated 9/4/68:

Edinburgh University: Played 34, won 30, points for 569 against 255, and no matches were drawn

Significantly this cutting contained the results of 354 top clubs in the UK and Ireland of which only four had won more matches, and only ten had lost fewer matches. As seasons go, it was one I was immensely proud to have been involved in.

NINE

Ian Smith had better play for Scotland after all the trouble he's caused me

The OBTC (Officers Basic Training Course) in Aldershot was designed to turn a bunch of student dentists into functioning army officers in around five or six weeks during August and September 1968.

Prior to our postings being announced I was asked whether I'd like to go to Wales.

Having been told as a group that we were now subject to the demands of the service, we would go where we were put.

I have always wondered if rugby had been an influence in this question but didn't dare to ask. I just said if it was possible I'd like to go to Germany, to BAOR (British Army of the Rhine), as it was known. To my surprise, my first posting was to the British Military Hospital in Münster, Westphalia, so I got what I wanted.

I had a few days at home before leaving, and felt like a game of rugby, so rang Tony Hogarth at Heriot's and he said he would fix it with the club. The next day I got a card to say I was in the 5ths, which I thought was a poor joke – considering the rugby I had been playing at university it was not unreasonable to think I would be picked for the seconds or thirds.

I was within two paces of picking the phone up to call off, because there was a friend's wedding at the weekend, when the phone rang. It was the Heriot's club secretary, asking if I could play for the 1st XV against Hawick on Saturday because Colin Blaikie was sick. Apparently, they had listed me for the 5ths because they knew Colin Blaikie was unlikely to be fit, and to bring me in from the lowly 5th XV would cause much less disruption than from a higher team.

Heriot's versus Hawick in September at Goldenacre was always one of the major matches of the season, if not the major match. This was classical excitement mixed with dread, and of course I accepted with alacrity despite the fact I hadn't really trained all summer. To play my last game of rugby in Scotland, or so I thought at the time, in such a prestigious game was too good an opportunity to miss.

As it turned out we beat Hawick by one point thanks to a glorious try by Tony Hogarth from an Edinburgh University miss-move we had only walked through in the warm-up. David Milne, also from the 1961/62 school 1st XV, kicked the conversion to hand us victory.

This was my first experience of using one of the university back moves without much rehearsal, with players new to it, and it was very definitely not the last time over the following two or three seasons. It really opened my eyes to what was possible because, thanks to Harry Rea, I could now explain how the miss-moves worked. Of course, playing with good footballers, they were easily able to time the passes well enough to make it successful.

My old schoolmate David Milne, who kicked the magnificent conversion which turned what would have been a defeat into a victory, thought he was kicking for a draw! Sadly for David, but critically for my future international prospects, I got all the credit for the match-winning try, which was grossly unfair on him.

The newspaper on Monday said: 'Ian Smith received a welcome home that made that accorded to the prodigal son appear positively hostile.'

That was true indeed, but prior to the match an old teammate from school spat on the ground telling me I didn't belong there, then after the match he was all full of praise, which I didn't like very much.

This, however, was probably the number-one hinge moment in my rugby life. Why? Because suddenly, having given that scoring pass, all seemed to be forgiven, in that I was accepted as a Herioter, which goes to show how much beating Hawick meant to the players and supporters at the time. Suddenly, I was rated as a full back who could well play for Scotland and become the seventh from the school to fill that position!

For the first time the press began to consider me a real contender for the full back's jersey, and it is interesting how much influence the press had in Scotland team selection in the 1950s, 60s and 70s – and press really didn't like it when they didn't have a clue who you were! In the 1960s, you had no real chance of selection for international honours if the rugby correspondents of the major newspapers hadn't picked you out as having potential. They were very much in control then of spreading the word about certain players' ability or inability, and to some extent that has never changed.

In the 1960s, if you wanted to know what was going on insofar as rugby in Scotland was concerned, then you needed to read the newspapers. Matches were on television, but only internationals, and never club matches, and international matches that were abroad in places like Paris were by and large only on the radio and I don't remember commercial television (ITV or STV) showing any rugby coverage at all in my youth. There was *Grandstand* all Saturday afternoon, and *Sportsnight with Coleman* during the week, and that was pretty well that. The lack of any television coverage without a doubt was the main reason that the miss-moves we developed as students remained a secret for so long. There were no coaches studying their next opponents and individuals in the opposition because there was no footage available. It is little wonder we were able to wreak havoc for over a season without any teams coming up with a plan to thwart us.

If you wanted to know what was going on in first-class club rugby, certainly as far as Scotland was concerned, you were therefore completely reliant on newspaper rugby columnists. If you were an ambitious player, you just had to hope at least one prominent rugby reporter liked you. The press approval then had to happen on a consistent basis a long way before selectors would ever pay any attention at all and, even then, there were no guarantees.

There was a system in existence in Scotland and basically it worked as follows. International teams were normally picked by a group of former players and internationalists known as the 'Big Six' or the 'Big Five'. As there were far more first-class matches going on in Scotland and one or two in England featuring exiled Scots than there were selectors, there was no way they could cover them all. This is where the newspaper reporters came into their element. On Sundays and Mondays, players and, I suspect, Scottish selectors as well, would scan the papers to read what the more highly regarded pundits had written. Friday's and Saturday's morning papers were equally worth checking and then as far as Edinburgh was concerned there was the 'Pink' and 'Green' Saturday evening papers as well.

Progress, or lack of progress, in your first-class rugby career could therefore easily be charted through the sports pages of the newspapers. Much of my research for this autobiography has been made easier by my father's fanaticism in that he cut out every press report he could find that was nice about me whilst I lived at home, and then by my curiosity when I moved down to England.

The first press reports I have relate to my debut in the school 1st XV in season 1960/61, when school matches were awarded two or three paragraphs in the *Evening Dispatch* and the *Edinburgh Evening News*. It was thrilling to read sentences like 'both full backs kicked and handled well' and to be mentioned by name was very much the exception.

From season 1961/62 when Tony Hogarth's 1st XV were very successful, and then David Boyd's 1st XV in 1962/63, the interest by the press in schoolboy rugby seemed to grow and there would often be more detailed reports in the local newspapers. Names were mentioned, whole teams were listed, and this coverage must have gone some way to selections for the Edinburgh Schools and then the Scottish Schools.

Games masters of course would have had an input, but their recommendations had a degree of bias, and could only be reinforced by other masters if they had seen individuals play. In the case of Heriot's, we didn't play some of the schools where players were selected, which must have added to the difficulties.

In other words, even at schoolboy level it was important to be seen and reported on by well-regarded rugby correspondents. Therefore, to attend a major rugby-playing school was almost a necessity, especially if you were lucky enough to be in the capital city.

When it came to senior rugby and first-class matches, the reports were no bigger than the school reports unless the side you were playing for or against was one of the leading sides in Scotland or a top-class side up from England, which was a rarity.

This explains the small number of Edinburgh University 1st XV reports in season 1965/66, and the huge number of reports in 1966/67 and 1967/68, when the university led the 'unofficial' championship in Scotland.

At Edinburgh University we were extremely fortunate that the doyen of Scottish rugby correspondents, Norman Mair, was a university rugby blue from the 1950s and a former international hooker. He wrote for *The Scotsman* and his reports were beautifully written and very perceptive, almost like essays – they were a joy to read. It was just reward for a long and distinguished career that Norman was elected to the Scottish Rugby Hall of Fame.

Norman was often to be seen at Craiglockhart and his reports were all devoured by the team afterwards. I was extremely fortunate that he seemed to like me, and as the seasons developed I was more and more encouraged by what he wrote and said, because he was such a good communicator at all levels. It didn't do me any harm at all that as secretary I was his first point of contact for team news, and his obvious delight at the resurgent form of his old student team jet-propelled our coverage in a widely read daily paper.

I would go so far as to say that I owe my one chance to be selected to play for Scotland to Norman's writing because of the high regard in which he was held by the Scottish Rugby Union. He closely and accurately monitored the improvement in the Edinburgh University team's performance and my own as firstly a defensive full back and then as an attacker.

When rugby fans began to realise the university side contained some real talent, mostly because of our results, but very definitely because of the great press, then selectors began to appear at matches. This led to the justified international recognition that Erle Mitchell and John Frame received. Even the Irish press took notice, and Harry Rea was deservedly given his Irish cap. It just remained a mystery that no one in England bothered to look at Ray Newton, who deserved to play for his country. Norman even checked out the slight possibility of Scottish ancestry, as I remember.

Another big fan of university rugby was Reg Prophit, who wrote for the *Evening Dispatch*, and the good press I received

The first Ian Smith left foot kick.

George Heriot's 1st Junior XV, 1955/56.
I'm in the back-row on the far left-hand side.

Four very proud Heriot's School 1st XV Colours Season 1962/63.
From left to right: Ian Smith, Bryan Lewis, Derek Lyle, Ian McCallum

The 1961/62 George Heriot's 1st XV. What a scary thought that this photo is
57 years old, and I can still remember it being taken. I'm seated, sitting second right.

EDINBURGH SCHOOLS XV v. GLASGOW 1961-62.

C.C. LAWRENCE.   D. FRASER.   G. MCGONIGAL.   B. LAIDLAW.   J. MCLEAN.   W.A. HOGARTH.
(WATSONS)   (R.H.S.)   (BRO'TON)   (R.H.S.)   (TRINITY)   (HERIOTS)

E. SCOTT.   W. NOBLE.   A. LAMONT.   G. MITCHELL.   R. CLARK.   J. ORR.   G. CONNEL.
(R.H.S.)   (BOR'MUIR)   (BOR'MUIR)   (MELVILLE)   (MELVILLE)   (R.H.S.)   (TRINITY)

I. S. G. SMITH.   I. ROBERTSON.
(HERIOTS)   (WATSONS)

Five future Scotland caps in this Edinburgh Schools team:
Erle Mitchell and Bob Clark from Melville College. Ian Robertson (with hair) from George Watson's, Gordon Connell from Trinity Academy, and myself. Ian and Gordon got their first caps as half backs on the same day. Note the polished boots and clean white laces.

Edinburgh Schools vs Midland Schools 1963 containing two future Lions in Chris Rea (front row, second left) and Gordon Connell (front right). I'm the second on the right in the front row.

1963 when Heriot's School 1st XV played Heriot's FP 1st XV. This was an annual fixture that is now impossible because of health and safety. I'm seated, fourth to the left.

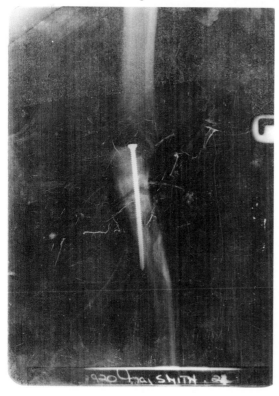

The x-ray of my 1967 fracture. I played for the rest of my rugby career with this and I still have the screw in my arm.

The Edinburgh University 1st XV, 1967/68.
I'm seated, just to the right of our captain.

Heriot's vs Hawick, September 1968. This turned out to be a major 'hinge' moment in my rugby career – if I hadn't played I'd never have been capped. I'm in the back row, second to the right.

Munster Medicals [BMH Munster] November 1968. I'm holding the ball in the front row.

The Guards Depot Pirbright Team in 1976. Again, I'm holding the ball in the front row.

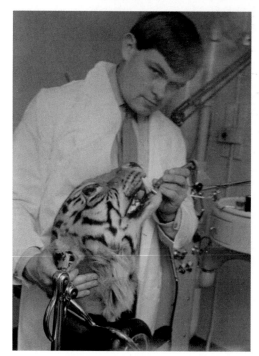

Occasionally dentistry was done in the Army.

Realising a childhood dream.

SCOTLAND v. SOUTH AFRICA
PLAYED AT MURRAYFIELD, 6TH DECEMBER 1969
SCOTTISH FIFTEEN

Mr R. P. Burrell   A. J. W. Hinshelwood   A. B. Carmichael   W. Lauder   G. L. Brown   P. K. Stagg   A. G. Biggar   J. N. M. Frame   I. S. G. Smith   Mr G. O. McInnes   Mr M. Joseph
Gala   London Scottish   West of Scotland   Neath   West of Scotland   Sale   London Scottish   Gala   London Scottish   Glasgow High School F.P.   Wales
Touch Judge   Touch Judge   Reserve

J. McLauchlan   C. W. W. Rea   I. Robertson   J. W. Telfer   R. J. Arneil   F. A. L. Laidlaw   D. S. Paterson
Jordanhill College   West of Scotland   Watsonians   Melrose   Leicester   Melrose   Gala
Captain

SCOTLAND 6   SOUTH AFRICA 3

The official team photo before my first cap.

Miss-one move against the Springboks 1969, with John Frame after his
beautifully timed pass. Sadly the ball is tucked under one arm!

from him may have been helped by the fact that he played tennis with my father before the Second World War!

It was still possible to make it to the top level playing for a lesser club providing you were given the opportunity at a higher level. One name that springs to mind is the legendary Scottish prop from the early sixties, David Rollo, who was a Lion in 1962. He played for a junior club, Howe of Fife, but his opportunities to shine came when he played for the North and Midlands against Edinburgh, Glasgow and the Borders. After that he had the Scotland trials to further his claims, when the Blues played the Whites in mid December followed a couple of weeks later by Scotland versus The Rest, after which the international team was announced.

David gave a young player called Jim Snape, who had just made his debut for North Midlands, some wonderful advice. Jim, sitting in the dressing room after the match, was saying how badly he himself had played when David interjected. 'Never say that, there'll aye be some bloody fool who thinks you played well, and it might be a reporter or a selector!'

How fortunate I was that the three wise old birds at Heriot's FP recommended Edinburgh University rugby to me, and the great good fortune that I had to be playing in a team who for two seasons astonished the world of rugby in Scotland.

What follows tracks my own progress as seen through the eyes of the press in Scotland between 1964 and 1968. This is not in any way meant to be conceited on my part, because it simply shows how the press can work for you and progress can be measured by the reports.

There seems to be an assumption that players who become internationalists have somehow or other stood out all the way through their rugby careers. This of course isn't true, as my Edinburgh University first-class debut shown here confirms.

Thursday, 5 November 1964, Edinburgh University 6 Co-Optimists 16, *The Scotsman*, by Norman Mair: *ISG Smith at full back had a bad game, but with more confidence and experience he will be an asset.*

In fairness, as you may have noted earlier, I was playing with an undiagnosed broken arm! It was to be a whole year before my next first-class match.

November 1965, Edinburgh University 15 Co-Optimists 19, *The Scotsman*, by a Special Correspondent: *Kemp was slightly better than Smith at full back, but the student showed any amount of courage and once his fielding is as safe as his kicking he will inspire as much confidence as Newton who was once again the spearhead of most of the Edinburgh attacks.*

I was desperate to be as good as Robbie Kemp who was the Edinburgh full back.

20 November 1965, prior to Bedford vs Edinburgh University, in the local Bedford paper: *Smith the full back is an excellent kicker but Briggs please note, is not always very happy with a high ball.*

My disturbing tendency to drop balls reared its ugly head again at an unfortunate time. This was the first game of our two-match tour, and to read that comment at breakfast knowing by reputation how good a kicker Pat Briggs was at fly-half for Bedford, made for a difficult morning!

22 November 1965, United Hospitals London 3 Edinburgh University 28, *The Scotsman*, by Norman Mair: *Even the chubby figure of ISG Smith was seen to be joining in the fun.*

My shape and general inference that I was unfit and slow does reoccur throughout my first-class career, but at least there was also an inference that we were trying to run the ball, although there was no real planning of how we could do this best.

25 November 1965, St Andrews University 11 Edinburgh University 8, *The Scotsman*, by Jack Dunn: *ISG Smith had a sound game at full back.*

13 December 1965, Edinburgh University 0 Cambridge University 11, *Daily Telegraph*: *At full back Smith fielded and kicked with the aplomb of a promising schoolboy who has at last settled into the senior game.*

Cambridge were on tour after the University Match and fielded ten blues in their side.

13 December 1965, *Daily Mail*, by Bruce Lewis: *As a last line of defence they had the great hearted Sidney Smith at full back. His sure fielding in the numbing wind and his long accurate touch-kicking turned back the light blues time and time again.*

13 December 1965, *The Scotsman*, report by Norman Mair: *The time has come to return Ray Newton, this gifted young footballer, to full back although the present occupant of the full back position ISG Smith mostly handled safely and often kicked very well.*

1965/66 season. Edinburgh University 0 Royal Dick Veterinary College 0, *Edinburgh Evening Dispatch*, by Reg Prophit: *When the Herioter ISG Smith matches his powerful punting off both boots with improved handling and mobility he could develop into a really reliable full back.*

No running with the ball mentioned here or in the last few reports!

March 1966, Edinburgh University 12 St Andrews University 3, *The Scotsman,* **by Jack Dunn:** *Any full back with the enterprise to press home an attack as successfully as Smith deserves a pat on the back.*

The first mention of running from full back before there was any real planning of how best to work it.

March 1966, Edinburgh University 14 Oxford University 6, *Daily Telegraph***:** *Once again Smith their young full back distinguished himself, apart from his forty-yard dropped goal.*

I had survived the season as the 1st XV full back without being dropped once and was beginning to get some nice comments about my defence and my kicking out of hand, as well as some attacking skill.

As I began to be a confirmed member of the 1st XV as secretary, so the press continued to be favourable, albeit still defensively, as season 1966/67 began and the university began to win matches consistently – in fact were unbeaten in Scotland.

October 1966, Edinburgh University 16 St Andrews University 0, *Daily Telegraph***:** *ISG Smith who gave his best display for the students this season, finding touch every time, tackling magnificently, and saving a certain score late on when he smothered . . .*

November 1966, Edinburgh University 0 Newcastle University 11, *Edinburgh Evening News,* **by Reg Prophit:** *Only immaculate kicking and courageous stopping by full back Ian Smith contained the visitors.*

Oxford and Cambridge universities were then to beat us in the space of five days.

***The Scotsman,* by Norman Mair:** *ISG Smith was not at his best but his advance this season was still readily apparent.*

It is only as we get towards the end of season 1966/67 that the press reports begin to differ.

There are two important things in terms of how rugby was played and how it was to develop. Firstly, the reports, insofar as my own performances are concerned, show a steady improvement. Nevertheless, all the reports focus on is the role of a full back as it was in the mid sixties. In other words, how good a full back's hands were, how well he kicked and found touch, and his defence. There is absolutely nothing to be read about the attacking element of the full back's game.

All this was to change as far as the reports of the Edinburgh University XV and myself went in the latter part of that season.

9 March 1967, Edinburgh University 20 Glasgow University 3, *The Scotsman,* by Jack Dunn: *Apart from performing his more routine duties in fielding and kicking in most reliable fashion, ISG Smith, Edinburgh's full back, had an influential part in the size of the victory through his readiness to take on the role of a fifth three-quarter and provide the overlap in handling bouts.*

Edinburgh University 20 Glasgow University 3, *Evening Dispatch,* by Reg Prophit: *And Smith at full back, apart from some thumping touch kicks, I have never seen play so brilliantly in attack. Three times the full back timed his break into the line so perfectly that the resultant tries were made to look all too easy.*

7 October 1967 (the start of the 1967/68 season), *Edinburgh Evening News*: *Smith's Flair. One of the most improved players in Scotland last season, Herioter Smith still has the elbow pinned but suffered no restriction of movement at Riverside. In fact, the full back whose timing of the break into the line is a feature of his play helped to make at least two of the tries against Jed.*

Edinburgh University 16 Dunfermline 5, as reported in the *Sunday Times*: *Smith made the running for the first try scored by McMillan, and 10 minutes from the end he joined the line at speed to make a clean break for a spectacular try.*

Edinburgh Evening News, **by Reg Prophit:** *Ian Smith is both sound and shrewdly adventurous with wonderful hands.*

February 1968, Gala 10 Edinburgh University 18, *The Scotsman,* **by Jack Dunn:** *Morgan's try was made possible by the timely help of ISG Smith whose happy flair for advancing from full back to make a fifth three-quarter has frequently stimulated his side's scoring power. To do such a thing once in a game is praiseworthy enough but the more commendable when it is repeated, as Smith despite a back injury, did a few minutes later.*

Gala 10 Edinburgh University 18, *Evening Dispatch*: *Ian Smith's flair for advancing from full back to make a fifth three-quarter is well known, but it was never better expressed at a time when it was most needed, when the students were behind 0-10 with not much more than twenty minutes to go, Smith twice in quick succession made the vital overlap to send Blair Morgan, his right winger over for tries.*

March 1968, *Edinburgh Evening News,* **by Reg Prophit:** *I have nothing but admiration for full back Smith's frequent incursions into* *the three-quarter line. No contemporary full back in the country times the creation of an overlap more skilfully than Smith, nor does the full back lose positional sense in an over anxiety to join the attack.*

Edinburgh University 23 Heriot's FP 0, *The Scotsman,* **by Norman Mair:** *The deceptively chubby and cherubic ISG Smith, himself a Herioter, had another grand match, not the least of his assets being the implicit faith his colleagues have in him. His has been a major influence in the University's recent exalted progress.*

March 1968, *Daily Mail,* **by Peter Donald:** *Smith had another fine game for the students. Cool and confident in defence, he is still always looking for an opening in attack, and apart from his try, he made the break which led to the opening score by winger Billy Wood.*

March 1968, Melrose 6 Edinburgh University 12, *The Scotsman,* **by Norman Mair:** *Smith had another magnificent match – one thump with his right foot into the wind being especially pleasing in one who was once reckoned as one footed as Long John Silver.*

March 1968, *Edinburgh Evening News,* **by Reg Prophit:** *How British Universities can continue to ignore the claims of Edinburgh's swashbuckling last line Ian Smith I just wouldn't know. Perhaps politics enters into rugby at all levels of the game!*

Preview of Co-Optimists versus Broughton FP, *Edinburgh Evening News,* **by Reg Prophit:** *Another highly attractive player making his debut in Co-optimists colours is Ian Smith the Edinburgh University full back. Smith has scored six tries for the students this season and carved out countless others.*

March 1968, Broughton FP 11 Co-Optimists 28, *Daily Mail:* *The Co-optimists had Smith Edinburgh University's attacking full* *back and Ming Campbell – who used his Olympic pace to run in four tries. Both were outstanding.*

As season 1967/68 ended I seemed to have developed a reputation as a running full back, without any real advancement. I played again for the Edinburgh A side in a repeat of the broken arm disaster of 1966, only this time I scored two tries. Sadly, Scottish Universities continued to prefer Geoff Allan of Glasgow University, and that was quite discouraging.

An extraordinary press report that came completely out of the blue, however, increased my profile. Norman Mair of *The Scotsman* asked me to meet him for a coffee to discuss the university year, in early March 1968. Little did I know what the result was to be.

It was thanks to two columns in *The Scotsman* which really propelled me into a spotlight, and alongside selection for the Co-Optimists began to make me be really noticed.

Broken arm has not deterred Smith. Fine Player, dedicated official.

Sec. Lieut. Ian Smith of the Royal Army Dental Corps has played 86 consecutive games for Edinburgh University 1st XV – an improbable feat in one who, since first matriculating, has twice broken his arm. Vice-captain of the Heriot's School XV in the last of his three years in the side – when he was also chosen for the Scottish Schoolboys XV – Smith tore ligaments at the start of the following season while playing against the school.

Consequently, his debut for the University's senior side was postponed till the Co-optimists match the next year, when a previous injury reasserted itself and a broken bone in his left arm was subsequently diagnosed – which made the unflattering Press opinion on his performance all the harder to bear.

Fit again, he was awarded his 'Green' the season after 1965/66. A year later he won his 'Blue' and made what so far was his only appearance for Scottish Universities. Alas at the end of the season playing for Edinburgh B XV against the Edinburgh and District Union he again broke his arm – the same bone but in a different place.

His rugby now seemed over; for, as an embryo dentist, he could ill afford a seriously damaged arm but Smith was not to be deterred; the bone was pinned and he was soon back in action at Craiglockhart.

His fielding technique was slightly modified, but to no lasting detrimental effect; indeed, so well has the deceptively cherubic University full back performed that he is one of five Edinburgh University players on the short-list for the British Universities match with the French Universities at Ebbw Vale – the others being Harry Rea, John Frame, David Boyle, and Patrick Irwin.

In fact, Smith 5 ft 11 in in height and 13st 9lb in weight – has quickened considerably since first making the University full back berth his own. In evidence of which one might cite the six tries he has scored himself this season and the 18 for which he has given the scoring pass.

His defence has tightened – although this was largely a matter of experience, for he has always enjoyed tackling, while the Heriot's record in 1961/62 – when in nineteen matches they only conceded a mere 37 points – would appear to indicate that even then, Smith was doing his stuff in that realm.

Less exclusively left footed than formerly, Smith has dropped some mighty useful goals, being especially prolific last season. His punting is of an unusually lofty trajectory, but it is a measure of its quality that his colleagues do not consider him inferior in that art to the thunderous Ray Newton.

This was of course written before the disaster that was the Hawick match but, prior to that, there was little doubt in my mind that some form of recognition wasn't to be far away.

Self-fulfilling prophecies happen and how quickly one can

go from the heights of optimism to the depths of depression. I began to feel certain that I couldn't really rely upon myself not to make really silly mistakes. Self-doubt has to be one of the most debilitating thoughts any sportsman can have, and I felt sure this would prevent my rugby career from going any further.

With the benefit of hindsight I now realise that one bad game and the small amount of publicity that ensued doesn't turn a good player into a bad player; it is only what goes on in your head as a consequence.

After saying all that, it seemed the Scottish rugby press hadn't written me off, even if I had!

At the time I had made what could well have been a fatal decision to abandon my first-class rugby dreams. I had decided to give up playing full back and escape to Germany with the Army when I found the newspapers beginning to put me in the frame for at least a Scottish trial.

Of course, the Heriot's versus Hawick match at Goldenacre had always been regarded as one of the big games of the season in Scotland. It was always so well covered by the press, and this was primarily the reason for the sudden interest.

September 1968, Heriot's FP 16 Hawick 15, *Sunday Times*, by Reg Prophit: *Apart from the pure realm of defence which he discharged soundly, Smith caused frequent havoc with well-timed counter attacks, and in a dramatic finish came into the line to send Hogarth in for a try.*

September 1968, *The Scotsman*, by Norman Mair: *The Heriot's backs swung right with their full back ISG Smith in the line but with the inside centre dropping out to give the move additional momentum against a defence with no time to align. Smith, as he had done so many times for Edinburgh University last season, timed his entry and pass to send WA Hogarth pounding over the line. Thus, Smith wound* *up an afternoon on which he had done much to erase the memory of an horrific evening against Hawick at the end of last season.*

September 1968, *Daily Telegraph*, by Ian Cameron: *Just two days earlier, in a rather more suave manner, Ian Smith the Heriot's full back had laid on the winning score for winger Tony Hogarth against Hawick with one of the most perfect intrusions into the line I have ever seen, crowned by a beautifully timed pass. Smith of course has always been noted for his intelligent link play with his three-quarters, and he either scored or helped to make at least 20 tries in his last season at Edinburgh University.*

That was very much that for my rugby in Scotland, as on the Monday following the Hawick match I was off to Münster in Westphalia, West Germany.

I had absolutely no intentions of playing rugby in Germany and, to be honest, it never crossed my mind that the British Military Hospital (BMH) Münster would have a rugby team, but it did.

Service rugby is quite unlike any other kind of rugby I was ever involved in and my experience began in September 1968. It sounded very impressive to be commissioned as Captain I.S.G. Smith Royal Army Dental Corps, but this seemingly exalted rank wasn't all it cracked up to be.

Things didn't start well when I was late for my flight to Düsseldorf. A very stroppy movements sergeant seemed to see by my discomfiture that I was completely wet behind the ears because he wouldn't let me on the aircraft, despite the fact that the flight hadn't taken off. He told me I would have to go back to my unit and rebook the flight, which could take a week. I panicked and paid not only for a civilian flight to Düsseldorf but also for a taxi to take me to Münster, to be told on arrival that if I had arrived a week later it wouldn't have mattered.

Military hospital rugby was very active in Germany in 1968, and BMH Münster, BMH Iserlohn, BMH Rinteln, BMH Hannover and BMH Berlin all ran rugby teams and competed for the Hospitals Cup. In addition, RAF Hospital Wegberg also appeared on the fixture list.

I very quickly found myself playing for BMH Münster at fly half and I was never again to play for a team where the enthusiasm was so infectious. This was my first experience of rugby where I wasn't trying to impress someone. Before, it was my father, a schoolmaster, the press, the captain of the side or the committee, and the release from pressure brought back the fun of rugby. It was more than a little help that the level was a long way from the standards of a Heriot's versus Hawick match or the university versus Gala, so I was to have things very much my own way – but that wasn't as easy as it sounds.

I had several invitations to play and even turned out as a guest for a Royal Green Jackets side after attending a regimental dinner night. What I do remember about the Royal Green Jackets game was that I was nearly sent off for the only time in my career. Every time I kicked the ball at fly-half, this wing-forward hit me late and knocked me over. Eventually, and very fed up, I asked the referee to intervene. At the very next scrum, I kicked the ball, was once again felled late, and the referee took no action, so I warned the player that if he did it again he could expect retaliation. At the next scrum I was knocked down late again, and as I got to my feet I was, I'm ashamed to say, about to kick the individual, and my foot was even raised in preparation, when I became aware of the referee two feet away and with his whistle poised.

After the match I approached the referee in the bar, who quite openly told me he would have sent me off for retaliation. I asked about all the late tackles and his comment was to the effect that it evened the game up. I was speechless. This was undoubtedly my introduction to Michael Green's *The Art of Coarse Rugby*.

Nevertheless, I have very fond memories of my brief rugby career in BAOR. This is even though I still carry the long-term effects of an injury to my left pinkie, caused by my sheer cowardice. We went to play at Forward Ammunition Depot Wulfen (FAD Wulfen) on a frosty day, with the pitch being quite hard in places. We had to take off our shoes when we entered the camp and wear slippers because of the danger of sparks. I'm certain to this day they were taking the mickey out of us. We were told it had been a German ammunition depot which was discovered when one of our bombers ditched some bombs and was nearly blown out of the sky. Apparently some of the German ammunition was still around, and not exactly stable after all the years that had passed.

Just as I was about to score a try, and because the pitch was frozen rock hard, I didn't want to skin my knees. Instead of diving, I touched the ball down with my left hand, just as someone jumped on it, splitting the tendon. As a consequence, for years afterwards if I bent the pinkie I had to use my other hand to straighten it and this meant always having to play with the pinkie strapped to the next finger for the rest of my rugby career. It did earn me a few beers over the years by challenging people to bend their pinkies right into the palm of their hand with the rest of their fingers and then keep it there when they straightened the rest of their fingers. Of course they couldn't but I could! Try it yourself.

As a dentist who worked standing up, as opposed to modern four-handed dentistry where everyone sits, I could guarantee at least once a day this finger would find its way up a patient's nose because I had no means of straightening it once it bent itself! Quite embarrassing but an interesting topic of conversation. Forty years later I still can't straighten my pinkie without help.

We played British Military Hospital Rinteln in the Hospitals Cup, and that was another levelling experience. They kicked off, a funny sort of kick that didn't go ten yards, I picked it up and scored under the posts. The conversion didn't even reach the bar, because the ball was both soft and wet. I complained to the referee, and he admitted, 'The ball's been in a bucket of water all night and deliberately half deflated so you wouldn't be able to kick it!' The game had to be stopped because I refused to play on, there was no ready replacement, and the pump had mysteriously gone missing!

Rugby in BAOR was proving a lot more entertaining than first-class rugby in Scotland! Sadly, my career in Münster didn't last long. I made some good friends in Rick Cooper and Paddy McHale. They were at that time private soldiers in the Royal Army Medical Corps (RAMC,) then both of them went on to have successful careers, and I think ended up as officers. The two of them got me into potentially serious scrapes and then got me out of them as well.

It was all very well for officers to play rugby with their soldiers, but socialising wasn't approved of. I have always used forenames names on and off the field when playing military unit rugby, trusting that when I encountered one of my teammates on duty that the normal military protocols would be observed.

On one occasion we were drinking in a downtown bar in Münster, when suddenly Rick and Paddy opened a window and threw me out into the snow for no apparent reason. It turned out it was out of bounds to British military personnel, and the Military Police had just come in the front door. It wouldn't have been good for my career as an officer to have been caught by them!

One of my last appearances for BMH Münster was on a Saturday immediately after a Regimental Guest Night. These are formal occasions in the officers' mess and everyone is dressed in their best, known as mess kit. As the newest and most junior officer I was what is known as 'Mr Vice' and amongst the quaint customs is the fact that 'Mr Vice' has to remain at the table, no loo breaks at all until the last guest has left.

I was plied with drink and can just about remember being put to bed. In the morning I had the hangover to end all hangovers, and the thought of rugby filled me full of horror. The officers mess seemed unusually busy that lunchtime and I realised that they were all there prior to watching the rugby. Normally we played in front of two men and a dog, so this was somewhat of a surprise. I realised why only after I made the mistake of running in a try from the halfway line, and promptly throwing up to a cacophony of jeers and laughter that this was exactly what they expected to see.

I still have the telegram from the BMH side when I was first capped against South Africa, and it is very precious to me because it always serves to remind me that the rugby played at that level is the heart and soul of the game.

In October/November of 1968, I received a letter from a senior officer ordering me to Düsseldorf to play in a trial for BAOR and although I had sworn not to play serious rugby again, an order was an order! I can't remember much about the trial on the Wednesday except I wasn't best pleased with the way I played as a full back. Fortunately, I played well enough to be told I'd be at full back three days later for the big match against Cape Town University who were on a European tour. The only problem was I had a dead leg, so much so I couldn't walk the next morning, never mind run.

I tried to run it off around the perimeter fence of the barracks we were staying in, but that was hopeless, so I retreated to the showers, and promptly sat in a hot bath for the next seven hours, with frequent applications of liniment. This was repeated on the Friday, and the Saturday morning.

By the time it came to the match, I could run okay and declared myself fit to play. One of the BAOR selectors was an army padre called Gerry Murphy, and he took me to one side and told me I had the ability to go far with my rugby, but I needed to learn how to dominate from full back. He spoke with the great authority of a man who is still regarded by the Irish as one of their great Test full backs.

We walked out on to the pitch and Gerry took me to all four corner flags. It was the quiet determination in his voice as he spoke about being a big man, exuding confidence, and being the dominant figure, always calling for the ball, making it mine, always finding touch, that struck me so profoundly.

Gerry told me I had to self-talk when I walked out onto the pitch before a match. The reason for going to the corners meant I would know exactly how the wind was blowing no matter where I was on the pitch. It was vital I tell myself how good I was, and that I was to be the rock the opposition foundered on. I hadn't realised before then that just because the wind seems set in one direction, if the pitch had a grandstand, that could introduce a swirl and therefore the wind could then vary according to where you stood on the pitch.

I have never forgotten the precious few minutes in the company of such a great man, and to my sorrow I never told him that, despite seeing him not long before he died a very few years ago.

Suddenly instead of dreading the occasion I was raring to go. Even being told the chairman of the Army selectors, Lt Col Roy Leyland, had come to watch me play didn't send me into my normal nervous twitching wreck. The transformation really was amazing.

One of the nice consequences of that match was playing opposite the Cape Town University full back whose name was Ian McCallum, and we became friends, meeting again in Edinburgh a few weeks later. I was even invited to his wedding, and he went on to become a Springbok full back on eleven occasions, playing against the Lions in 1974. Ian then went on to have a great career and is a man of some renown in South Africa.

I must have played well enough, because I was posted soon afterwards to England.

My top boss was the Deputy Director Army Dental Services BAOR. At that time, it was a Scottish colonel named Ken Galloway who later became the Major General Director Army Dental Service. He complained bitterly that he had been called at home on a Sunday by Lt-General Mervyn 'Tubby' Butler who was GOC (General Officer Commanding) 1 BR Corps. This call was short and to the point, telling him there was a dental officer called Ian Smith who was to be posted home within the next seven days to southern England, so he could play for the Army. As you might guess, this did not make me at all popular with Colonel Galloway! He had to find me a place to work and someone to move to Germany at very short notice in my stead.

Colonel Galloway apparently was heard to say later, 'Ian Smith had better play for Scotland after all the trouble he's caused me!'

It was very strange to discover much later that Ken Galloway was at St Andrews with my father and they had played tennis together for the university. Not for the first or last time in my life has sport made connections through the generations.

What I didn't know was that even in my absence from the Scottish rugby scene, my name had continued to crop up in newspaper articles in Scotland, but now quite differently from my recent university rugby career. One or two rugby correspondents were beginning to suggest I should at least be chosen for one of the Scotland international trials.

It seems difficult to believe nowadays that each country had trial matches before the international teams were selected. These normally took place in late December and early January in Scotland, and the first was Blues versus Whites, with the Blues being the more likely candidates for the international team.

Sometimes the teams were Probables versus Possibles, and the second trial was Scotland versus The Rest. Players could be promoted or demoted during the trial. There were reserves in attendance who could be brought on, and to some extent it wasn't unlike the weekly practice matches at school. Having said that, it took place at a nearly empty Murrayfield under the accusing glare of the selectors, and the echoing clatter of the seats as they dropped down.

In my youth, my father, who had a totally unreasonable and vindictive hatred of a great Scotland fly half called Gordon Waddell, used to position himself in the stand immediately behind the selectors box and abuse Waddell in some basic Anglo-Saxon language at the trials. The point of this was that Gordon's father, Herbert, was one of the selectors, known as 'the Big Five'. Herbert was a very famous ex-Scotland fly half in his own right, but my father knew he had won when eventually Herbert turned round, stood up, and asked him to be quiet. This was regarded by my father as a major triumph.

Being talked about as a potential trialist only came about because of my one successful game for Heriot's.

September 1968, *Daily Mail*: *History could be repeating itself next month when the Scottish Selectors name their teams for the first trial at Murrayfield on October 26th.*

Last year Rodger Arneil was flown over for the first trial. This season it could be the turn of Ian Smith the former Edinburgh University full back who starred in Heriot's exciting 16–15 victory over Hawick at Goldenacre last Saturday . . . It was Smith's attacking talents that won the match.

December 1968, *Evening Dispatch*, **by Reg Prophit:** *Ian Smith Plays for Army XV.*

Ian Smith, Edinburgh University's adventurous full back and secretary for the past few seasons, who played a great game on his one and only appearance for Heriot's FP against Hawick at Goldenacre in September, has been captaining the British Military Hospital XV in Munster, Germany.

An officer in the Royal Army Dental Corps, Smith has been scoring regularly with the boot and was recently watched by Colonel Roy Leyland, the former England back who flew specially to Dusseldorf for the occasion

As a result, the Herioter will be playing for the British Army against Blackheath in London next Saturday, after which he will be coming home on New Year leave.

Many good judges believe Smith was unlucky not to be chosen in opposition to Colin Blaikie the Heriot's internationalist for the final trial at Murrayfield next week.

December 1968, *The Scotsman*, by Norman Mair: *Smith could put bite into Scots XV.*

No I think the full-back the selectors would most like to have a look at is ISG Smith a dentist now serving in the Army in Germany.

Anyway, as things would have it I pulled a hamstring shortly after I was posted, so couldn't even play for the Army for a while.

Pulling the hamstring was one of the least pleasant experiences in my rugby career. The Army were playing Surrey under the lights at Esher, and I had travelled down from Edinburgh after visiting my parents. It was, at that point, a unique experience to use a railway warrant as I was travelling on service matters.

I had to go to Edinburgh Castle where I found myself in front of a brigadier called Frank Coutts, a most delightful man, and with, at that stage, little dealings with senior officers, I wasn't sure what to expect. We had a long chat about rugby; he had played for Scotland immediately after the Second World War, and in fact was later to become president of the Scottish Rugby Union.

I had a sleeper ticket to go back to Edinburgh but having been forced to leave the pitch halfway through the first half, no one came to my assistance and I had to hobble off the pitch to the changing room. It isn't more than a few yards, but as anyone with a torn hamstring will agree, one step is torture. The large bath was in the process of being filled and was only ankle deep but the water was scalding hot, and it was almost impossible to raise my leg to get in and out.

The walk to Hersham station was agonising, then getting from Waterloo to King's Cross for the sleeper train via the tube was a journey I have tried my best to forget. To add insult to injury, I was on the top bunk on the sleeper, and my travelling companion was already in bed and asleep, so there was no chance of a swop.

My father met me at the station, with that kind of look that only parents can give when their offspring are obviously in serious pain. This was my first experience of a muscle tear, and it wasn't to be my last. It is the psychological impact that it makes, and I never felt totally confident again sprinting flat out, but perhaps that was because I didn't have the correct immediate post-injury treatment.

The injury was in some respects a blessing in disguise, however, for two reasons. The first was that I was able to travel up to Edinburgh over a number of weekends to rescue my engagement to Maureen with whom I had an on-off relationship over a number of years. Secondly, the weather was so bad with snow and frost that a number of rugby matches were cancelled, meaning I wasn't missing much by being injured.

One horrendous Friday, I drove up to Edinburgh because once again Maureen had decided to call off the wedding which was due in April 1969.

There are two ways to drive into Scotland on the east coast, the first is up the A1, which I hated, or the A68 inland, which is hilly with lots of switchbacks. It was dark on the Friday evening and snowing quite hard as I drove north on the A68 in my big left-hand-drive Mercedes 220Sb.

The lorry in front got slower and slower, and because of the heavy snow I couldn't see to overtake, and then suddenly it stopped. The driver appeared at my window and asked me in fairly basic terms, 'Where the hell do you think you are going?' When I told him I was going to Edinburgh he told me in no uncertain terms that I wasn't because he was a snow plough! It took him twenty minutes to cut a space so I could turn and re-route myself.

When I came south on the Sunday it was a beautiful clear frosty night and the A68 over Carter Bar was absolutely deserted, and although there was snow on the road it wasn't too bad. It was only when I got to Corbridge, and I had to move oil drums and planks blocking the road, that I saw the sign which read 'ROAD CLOSED. The A68 is blocked many miles ahead'.

I didn't have a map in the car so I managed to get slightly lost ending up on what I think was the unopened M40. There were plastic cones which I gently pushed aside, and I thought no more of it until I was pulled over by a police officer at seven in the morning in Farnborough. He was convinced I was a drunk driver because there were two cones stuck under the car, but he did see the funny side of it when I told him the tale of my weekend.

When my rugby restarted I began to be extremely busy, playing for the Army, Combined Services, London Scottish Extra A, Hampshire, and the RAMC. These were the teams I was to spend my time with in seasons 1969/70, 1970/71 as well as the tail end of 1968/69.

The RAMC consisted of not only medics but dentists as well, and they played against other corps sides such as the Royal Corps of Transport (RCT) Royal Engineers (RE), Royal Artillery (RA), Royal Electrical and Mechanical Engineers (REME), Royal Army Education Corps (RAEC) and they all had their strengths. RE had Hamish Bryce, a Cambridge blue and the Army and Combined Services captain, who was unlucky enough to have to compete with Ian McLauchlan, the 'Mighty Mouse', for the Scotland jersey. He was to win just the one cap but deserved many more. The RCT had John McDonald, Scotland prop and goalkicker extraordinaire, who was a Watsonian and later became a major general. The RA had Andy Hoon, later to become a brigadier.

REME had the legendary David Spawforth, a scrum half who should have played for England but his lowly army rank did not fit with the English selectors. Sadly, David is no longer with us, but was described as the best scrum half never to play for England. There was always a feeling in the early seventies that to be a serviceman and play for England you had to be an officer. This may be untrue, but Peter Eastwood, another great army second row stalwart of the Royal Army Pay Corps, never played for England, and was commissioned too late in his career. Sadly, Peter is also no longer with us, but he and David remain two shining examples of the snobbery that existed in the RFU at that time.

Curiously, the Royal Air Force didn't have the same problem, and Peter Larter played for England whilst Billy Steele was picked for Scotland without being officers.

I digress again, because the RAMC were fortunate enough to be able to choose Mick Molloy and Al Moroney, both Irish internationals, Richard Rea who captained London Irish, Charlie Bale who played for Combined Services and, I think, for the Barbarians as well, plus myself, which meant we had a strong side, and I don't remember us losing a match.

The hurried posting home to England found me in a tiny dental centre in Aldershot, with a major in charge who was an extremely patient man, because the demands of rugby meant I was often absent.

Living in Farnborough meant I was eligible to play for Hampshire, although they had a good naval officer at full back called Peter Golding. I wasn't certain I would be chosen, but managed to make the side, although we didn't win much in the way of matches.

As I remember, we were in a county championship group which included Sussex, Eastern Counties and Surrey. I have only one memory of the Surrey match and that was dislocating a rib cartilage, quite one of the most painful things in my life. The army kindly fixed me up to see Bill Tucker at the Park Street Clinic. I found myself sitting next to Richard Todd, the famous actor, who to my surprise asked what had happened to me and was very chatty.

In my innocence I had no idea what was about to happen. Stripped to the waist I was injected right into the injury with a corticosteroid solution. The pain was so intense that the tears ran down my face; I have never experienced pain like it before, and only once since.

In fairness it worked and vitally so because it allowed me to continue playing shortly afterwards, and subsequent non-rugby rib cartilage dislocations have taken months to heal.

Possibly my outstanding memory of Hampshire rugby was a gentleman called Gerald Penn-Barrow who was certainly a committee member, and possibly secretary. He was most incredibly generous, wining and dining players who had travelled some distance to matches, even putting us up in nice hotels.

After one such match against Surrey, after a few drinks and some wine, the group of players realised how close we had come to an upset. We concluded that had we held on to a couple of passes, and not missed a couple of tackles or lost a couple against the head at crucial scrums, we could well have beaten the mighty Surrey. They as ever were jam-packed with internationals, everyone playing for a first-class club, whereas we in Hampshire had at the most a couple of players playing first-class rugby.

Imagine our amazement on reading the *Daily Telegraph* the next morning at breakfast and discovering we had shipped nearly fifty points!

My only other Hampshire memory was the very rare honour of captaining Hampshire against Sussex, who were skippered by R.D.V. Knight, later to be president of the MCC. That was only the third time I had ever captained a team in my life.

The two 'big' matches for the Army are the Inter-Service Championships against the Royal Navy and the Royal Air Force, with both matches played at Twickenham. Prior to that the Army had an impressive fixture list playing teams like Harlequins, so although I had failed to make an impact at London Scottish, playing for the second seconds (3rds), I was still getting regular first-class rugby with the Army.

Selection for Combined Services was based almost entirely on the Inter-Service matches, so showing good form against the Royal Navy and the Royal Air Force was important.

My father continued to send me down from Edinburgh several press cuttings as I confirmed my place in the Army XV to play the Royal Navy at Twickenham, so I was as pleased as punch to be chosen.

February 1969, *The Scotsman*, by Norman Mair: *Scots Rugby Players on the fringe*
Ian Smith formerly of Edinburgh University and Heriot's FP and now of the Army who before his recent injury has added successful goal kicking to his merits as an attacking full back.

March 1969, *Sunday Times***:** *Scotland own such full backs as the former Edinburgh University full back Ian Smith who has blossomed in the Army as a goal kicker while confirming his reputation as a master at contriving the attacking overlap.*

There was a level of violence in Army and Combined Services matches that I had never experienced before or since. The one game that stands out above all others was the Army versus Navy game in 1970 at Twickenham. Unlike today, Twickenham was less than half full but the noise and aggro was almost overwhelming. The Navy came out with all guns blazing and, as I remember, reduced us to thirteen players within the first few minutes.

The first high ball I waited under never got closer than ten feet before I was taken out. I have been nervous more often than not, but only really scared on that one occasion. The chief perpetrator was Leigh Merrick with whom I was to play a few times for Combined Services and against at Richmond. I should add that off the field he was the most charming of men, but when up against the Army in Royal Navy blue, he was a totally different animal. We were well and truly beaten that day, but then fifteen will nearly always beat thirteen!

We beat the RAF in a terrific game at Twickenham and I found out later that George Burrell, the former Scotland full back and national selector, had been at the match. I felt I hadn't done too badly, in fact well enough to be picked for the Combined Services side to play the French Armed Forces.

At the time I was playing for the Army in season 1968/69 there were still current, future and ex-internationals playing inter-service rugby. Even the Army selectors were virtually all ex-internationals. Colonel Roy Leyland was the Army's chairman of selectors who first watched the BAOR match against Cape Town University. Brigadier T.G.H. Jackson played for Scotland in the 1940s, Padre Robin Roe played for Ireland, Norman Bruce hooked many times for Scotland, and Mike Hardy played fly half for England, so there was a good amount of expertise there.

Playing for the Army side were Irish internationals Mick Molloy and Al Moroney in the pack, and England trialist Peter Eastwood. We were captained by Hamish Bryce, who was to win a Scottish cap. Our hooker was the late Gerry Miller, who played for Harlequins, and a most entertaining man. I have never seen a less likely hooker than Gerry, who was picked on a lot, as he didn't look like your average front row forward, and in those far-off days before rugby became sanitised he was frequently punched and kicked. His response, however, was classic:

'You're going in my little book.'

'What do you mean?'

'In five years' time, when you've forgotten all about this, you'll go down on a ball, and then I'll kick your fucking head in. Revenge is a dish best served cold.'

I saw Gerry's little book after more than one match, as he gleefully scored a name out . . . We just don't breed characters like that anymore.

The Combined Services team to play the French Armed Forces in Angers in France contained four internationalists in Peter Glover, who played on the wing for England, Peter Larter, the England second row, Mick Molloy and Al Moroney, and three who were yet to be capped in Hamish Bryce, Billy Steele, who became a Lion in 1974, and finally me.

Although we were a strong side we lost, but it was another step up the shaky ladder to higher honours.

The game was shortly before I was to be married to Maureen, which is the only way I can remember when it was, because I bought her a perfume that was to remain her favourite. I had gone shopping for a perfume and literally had two arms drenched in perfume as I tried to decide which one I liked the best. I smelled for days.

We were taken round the Cointreau factory, and warned by Air Commodore Bob Weighill who was, I think, our president, not to partake of the product, which we managed to resist. However, we were also warned by our guide that the fumes could make us slightly tipsy on their own, which was quite right.

I was somewhat staggered to see my name and photograph in one of the French newspapers, and my first experience of playing against a French side was traumatic in that I was punched in the face, suffering a split lip, which rapidly turned to a massive mouth ulcer. The only food available whilst waiting to fly home was thick-crusted French stick which was agony to eat. Apart from the cracked lip and the general level of violence, the only other thing I can remember was being awarded the 'best player'.

It was about this time that my father rang to tell me I was being talked about as a possible for the forthcoming Scotland tour to Argentina. Impending marriage would have excluded me from the Argentina tour and, in any case, I was never approached, but married bliss was to hand me another challenge I could not have foreseen.

TEN

Just give me the one chance to show how good I can be

Maureen and I were married on 26 April 1969 and over that summer my weight ballooned to over fifteen stones. A simple sentence, but one that hides the fact that I was drinking seven pints of full cream milk a day and was eating a full English fried breakfast every morning.

We had inherited the Smith family refrigerator, which in 1969 was still considered a luxury item. It was a huge fridge, with a small central freezer only for ice, and on each side the milk would stand keeping it ice cold. I just loved milk, and still do. In fact, I once drank a whole crate at school, which consisted of twenty-four one-third of a pint bottles, meaning a gallon of milk. I remember having to leave a French class three times during the forty-minute period.

I started training for the rugby season in August, which was quite normal in the late 60s. Until I was asked to play for London Scottish 1st XV against Headingley I thought I was getting reasonably fit. Their young fly half called Ian McGeechan soon gave me a reality check. Their wing scored three tries and I struggled to get across the pitch. This was followed by an Army match against Devon when I thought I'd played quite well, dropping a goal, kicking a couple of penalties, even scoring a try. Afterwards Colonel Jack Dalrymple, a wise old bird, who was secretary of the Army Rugby Union, told me in no uncertain terms I was too fat and unfit. He said well-informed people thought I had a promising future, but it wasn't going to happen unless I lost at least a couple of stones.

His exact words were short in number and brutally frank: 'You need to lose a lot of weight and lose it quickly if you want to play for Scotland.'

This certainly galvanised me and with Maureen pregnant with our first child, and the fact that we had our first television set, conspired together to start me on a weight loss program. I should add that as a young captain in the Royal Army Dental Corps, we were too young to get an official army quarter, but able to get a sub-standard quarter outside Farnborough in Hampshire, near Minley Manor, called the King George V Cottage. It was an old semi-detached house with a big private garden. Our nearest building was some four hundred yards away and was called the Crown and Cushion pub.

What saved my bacon was an early evening BBC programme called *Nationwide*, hosted by Michael Barratt, which featured a low carbohydrate diet. I found this easy to follow and living out in the country with lots of fields and woodland tracks, plus owning my first dog, Robbie, a cross Alsatian Labrador, meant I was running every day. I was also training at least twice a week and playing most Wednesdays and Saturdays. This meant by the time it came to late November I had shed over two stone.

During that time, I continued to play for the Army, Hampshire and London Scottish 3rds, my poor showing at Headingley having cast me into the rugby wilderness as far as they were concerned.

I was fortunate enough to play once in Edinburgh for the Co-Optimists against the university, which turned out to be my last club game ever in Scotland, so it was rather fitting that it was a repeat of my first-ever first-class match. I was luckily able to come into the line and give a couple of scoring passes to Gil Borthwick, who I had played with at school. He was talented and athletic enough to play for Scotland but sadly he never did, in fact dying tragically young.

The match kind of reminded rugby followers in Scotland, and the international selectors, that I still existed, which was to be of crucial importance come the end of November 1969.

I was extremely fortunate to captain the Co-Optimists side, not for any other reason than traditionally their captain was always the player who had played the most and had never captained the side before. On that occasion it happened to be me.

The tie at that time was a dark-blue tie with what appeared to be a white sphinx in the middle. Playing entitled you to buy one, but if you were captain you were presented with a tie with a circle around the sphinx. I am proud to say I also played and captained the Hong Kong Co-Optimists, and have a tie with the white sphinx and the initials HK underneath. I feel privileged to be one of a small band of players entitled to the three ties, and will always be grateful to George St Claire Murray for the opportunity to play against the university at such a crucial time for me.

I think the sentiments of the title of the chapter probably sums up better than anything the dreams and aspirations of any sportsman or woman. However, we mustn't ever expect the one chance to come around again. All we can ever ask for is one opportunity to prove that we are good enough to achieve our dreams, and I was to be given that chance on 26 November 1969.

Combined Services were asked to provide the opposition to what was essentially a Scotland XV to give them a run-out prior to playing the Springboks in early December.

I found myself chosen for Combined Services, which was exciting; it would give me the chance to see my parents, test myself against the best Scotland had to offer, and that was about that, until I arrived in Edinburgh.

What I hadn't appreciated was that there was somewhat of a crisis in terms of full backs. Colin Blaikie, the current full back, was injured; Hugh Penman, possibly his understudy, was unwell; so the Scottish full back was going to be Gordon Macdonald from London Scottish.

My father greeted me the day before with the comment, 'You have a big chance tomorrow to impress the selectors.'

I don't think for one second he thought (and I certainly didn't think) this was any more than a chance to at least put myself in the frame for the future.

He went on to tell me about the full back crisis and how Gordon Macdonald hadn't looked very good in the Scottish trial, but the selectors were very keen to pick him because his one cap had been as a three-minute substitute under controversial circumstances. Apparently, Gordon had run on when Chris Rea got injured against Ireland but before the doctor had said Chris was unfit to continue, so he should have waited. As Gordon was in his thirties and unlikely to get a better chance with only three minutes to go, I'm sure I'd have done the same thing. Understandably there was a desire to see him get properly capped, although there were doubts about his mobility and his goal kicking. It was his to lose, and I was just looking forward to the opportunity to play without giving much thought to my own chances. Nevertheless, just to get the chance to see how I could cope at this level was exciting enough, without there being any great tension involved.

That was until the morning of the match, and reading the daily newspapers dramatically changed my thoughts.

Daily Telegraph

Playing against Macdonald on that occasion will be Ian Smith who, since leaving Edinburgh University has had considerable representative experience with Combined Services, BAOR, in Germany, the British Army, and Hampshire.

As an attacking full back, he has played one or two games at fly-half, and even on the wing, and he is a prolific scorer with the boot. The clash between Smith and Macdonald with certainly command the selectors' attention.

Glasgow Herald

Fortunately another candidate for the full back position will appear before the selectors at Murrayfield this week. The Combined Services for Wednesday's match have chosen Ian Smith formerly of George Heriot's School and Edinburgh University, now serving with the Royal Army Dental Corps and playing county championship rugby for Hampshire. He follows in the Heriot's tradition as a sound full back and has, in addition a sound eye and judgement for the overlap.

Scottish Daily Express

Ian Thomson, Ken Scotland and Colin Blaikie are three of the best full backs who have played for Scotland in post-war years. They have one thing in common – an education at George Heriot's School in Edinburgh.

Today another product of this "school for full backs" has the chance to show the Scottish selectors he is ready to follow in their footsteps. Army officer Ian Smith formerly of Heriot's and Edinburgh University is the "last line" of the Combined Services against the Scottish Districts. When at University Smith was one of the fastest full backs in Scotland with a notable attacking flair. If he outshines Macdonald today who has obvious limitations the "Big Six" must be sorely tempted to give him his chance.

The Scotsman

For their full back Ian Smith the pressures have been building up which would presumably make a good performance that much more relevant – though heaven knows playing full back in an almost empty Murrayfield under the accusing scrutiny of the national selectors has probably more in common with the goldfish bowl than the international arena. Now 25 Smith has slimmed down somewhat from the cherubic young man I first remember not in his days as the Heriot's and Scottish Schoolboys fullback but as a fresher at Edinburgh University.

That day I recall being a little critical of his ability – accurately enough, but possibly a little harshly, since it transpired later that he was playing with a broken arm.

A goodish tennis player in his day, with the kind of eye for a ball which that suggests, Smith had, with the exception of one horrific evening at Hawick, a brilliant last season at Edinburgh University. That season one had to go outside rugby to Parkhead, and Tommy Gemmill to find a full back who came up to attack to equally devastating effect.

However to the selectors Gordon Macdonald is clearly the man in possession and Smith will have to be very obviously the better man if at this late stage he is to force his way into the team against South Africa – a situation which in a sense ought to help him for he has the less to lose.

All of that made for an interesting breakfast on that fateful Wednesday. Comments like this just go to show how uninformed the press can be. I would have bet a lot of money that the 1967/68 University side would have beaten any of the teams they mentioned I had been playing for. In other words, it looks impressive, listing all these teams, but that was a lot different to the reality. In fact, I had played very little decent rugby since leaving university, and now I was seriously concerned I might show myself up as not being fit enough or good enough. My parents were magnificent that morning, reminding me how much I deserved the chance, and the number of times I had been disappointed at not being selected for the likes of Scottish Universities. This was my moment they told me, and of course it was.

When I look back now, I can only think of the words that every little boy who aspires to play for Scotland uses in his prayers: 'Just give me the one chance to show how good I can be.'

That was exactly what I was getting.

This was probably the only day of my whole rugby career where I wasn't in the least nervous. It was almost as if I knew this was my destiny, and now it was entirely up to me to show I was good enough – my one moment in time. This was the one chance I had dreamed about for most of my life and now it was actually happening. Without ever consciously thinking about it, I'd done everything possible to be ready. All the kicking and catching practice I'd put in just because I loved it so much.

Potentially I was eighty minutes away from a Scotland cap and if that was to happen it was entirely up to me. My dream was so close I could almost touch it. As my parents had said in the morning, that over a very long period of time I practised for this moment, and now it had arrived. What they said was that if I got it right I'd be famous forever as the seventh Herioter to play full back for Scotland.

I find writing about it extremely emotional even though it was almost fifty years ago because that day changed my life forever.

There are rugby matches that stay fixed in the memory, where you can remember everything that happened. This was not the case on 26 November 1969. I know the result was Scottish Districts 31 to Combined Services 12, and I scored all twelve points for Combined Services, but I have only got snapshot memories of moments in the match.

The first was being handed a questionnaire in the dressing room, and on asking what it was about, being told it was for the international programme.

Secondly, being hauled to the side by cameramen as we ran out on to the pitch to be photographed, which was a bit disconcerting.

Thirdly, I remember Gregor Campbell, our fly half, kicking a couple of balls upfield and Gordon Macdonald dropping them, and I hadn't even touched the ball at this point. It was my good fortune that Ian Robertson at fly half for the Scottish Districts wasn't primarily a kicker.

Fourthly, I missed my first kick at goal, and then we were awarded a penalty thirty-five yards out to the left of the posts and about a foot in from touch. I dug my hole, placed the ball, walked back to then realise that Jim Telfer was hurt, and the game had been stopped. I knew I had to kick the goal, and the left-hand side of the posts was harder for me as a left-foot kicker. Tense doesn't do justice to my feelings during the two long minutes that passed, and just at that moment a photographer interrupted my reverie by taking a picture. This was the one that appeared in the first international programme against South Africa, so it was no wonder I looked a bit thoughtful. Luckily, I kicked the goal, and that is the last memory I have of the match. It was only later that evening as we were about to board the night sleeper to London that I was handed the next morning's copy of *The Scotsman*. My heart leapt about three feet, it was hard to believe that I might be so close to selection.

'Ian Smith may have kicked himself into Scotland XV', by Norman Mair

Since most certainly it is the position currently causing the selectors most anxiety one should perhaps begin with the full backs. Gordon

Macdonald – his knee bandaged and looking once or twice laboured to the point of lame – made, poor fellow, more basic errors in the one afternoon than he has sometimes made in a whole season for London Scottish and Middlesex.

Smith, heartened no doubt by the sight of Macdonald spilling a couple of catches before he had been called upon to do anything, had an excellent game, marred only by missing Hinshelwood during a rather untidy few minutes towards the end.

Slightly – but never awkwardly – one footed, Smith mostly fielded cleanly and kicked soundly, putting a seal on a memorable display by coming into the line absolutely perfectly to score a copybook try.

In addition, he kicked three penalty goals, and on the afternoon was the most successful goal kicker. Alternating between the London Scottish 2nds and 3rds Smith has had little chance this season in club rugby, although he has had plenty of quite good stuff with Hampshire and the Army.

I gather the selectors have not yet seen a great deal of him this winter and the evidence of yesterday's match, convincing though it was and even allowing that they know him of old, is not all that much on which to award a first cap. But this of course is now something of an emergency, while those of his rivals who are still in one piece and within reach have done rather more to play themselves out than in. He would be my choice – but I would not be surprised if the selectors want to see him again on Saturday.

As things happened, the London Scottish 3rd XV match on the Saturday was cancelled, which may have been just as well for my selection prospects!

Other press comments included:

Evening Dispatch by Reg Prophit
If ever a man stole the show, right under the noses of the selectors, it was Ian Smith the former Edinburgh University and Heriot's full

back who scored all 12 points for the Combined Services beaten 12-31 by Scottish Districts at Murrayfield.

Quite apart from his scoring feat of a beautifully taken try and three penalty goals, Smith's fielding in the bitter cold was a feature. He did not knock on once in the game and was eminently safe in all other departments.

It would be a remarkable turn of events if the 25-year old Herioter were to by-pass the trials on his way to a first cap against the Springboks a week on Saturday. It has been said that the "Big Six" were desperately anxious to give Gordon Macdonald, the London Scot a genuine cap to add to the one he received for five minutes as a substitute against Ireland last season.

But that would be no valid reason at all. Merit surely is the only yardstick for a cap, and if Smith did not do enough to play himself in yesterday, then just as surely Macdonald did plenty to play himself out.

Both Macdonald and Smith are a little one-footed, but the Londoner looked positively ponderous at times and one shudders at the thought of him having to chase diagonals from the Springbok fly-half.

Another ironic feature of the situation is that since Macdonald is the current London Scottish captain, Smith has had to accept a modest role with the Exiles reserves. Smith has in fact played for the Scottish 1sts, 2nds, and 3rds this season as well as winning two county caps for Hampshire.

There were a number of other Scottish press reports in much the same vein, so as you can imagine I did not sleep too well on my way south, or for that matter during the next few nights either.

ELEVEN

But who are you?

It was Sunday, 30 November when the telephone began to ring at home. First it was my father who told me he thought I was to be a reserve for the match because the SRU wanted my address, and then came a call from a well-known *Daily Mail* rugby columnist in England called Terry O'Connor. 'Congratulations,' he boomed down the line after informing me of my selection. 'But who are you?'

He told me I seemed to have come from nowhere, so I gave him some background, and he seemed happy enough. I can't remember much of the conversation apart from congratulating me on my selection, but his query about who I was isn't a surprise – after all, not many people get capped from their club 3rd XV.

I am still certain that the English press believed I was an overnight success, and of course such things are very unlikely, if not impossible. Success never comes overnight; it might appear suddenly, but only after what may be years of invisible honest toil where success and failure week in, week out are the only yardsticks you have to measure yourself by, until you are noticed by a rugby correspondent of a major national newspaper.

In my case, I could hardly expect the English rugby correspondents to have a clue who I was because they had little reason, and no evidence at all, to pick me out. I was just a Scotsman who had played less than one year in England with little or no success. The years of slowly climbing a ladder from small boy rugby, to school first XV rugby, to being involved in one of the most successful club sides in Scotland meant nothing to an English rugby correspondent.

The fact is that typically England really couldn't have cared less about what was going on in Scotland in the 1960s and this didn't only apply to rugby. Some things haven't changed nearly sixty years later. You won't find much about rugby in Scotland on the sports pages in English newspapers unless, of course, Edinburgh or Glasgow are playing against a major English club. Terry O'Connor's words therefore were hardly a surprise on that front either.

I have been called many things in my life, possibly the funniest was when another well-known English rugby correspondent named me as one of the six worst international rugby selections of all time. He may well have been right!

The unkindest is to be called 'lucky' and that was a comment I was to hear many times in the weeks and months following my first cap for Scotland. Lucky to be picked because the best three or four full backs were unavailable, and lucky to score a try, kick a penalty and score all of my country's points in my first international.

I don't believe in luck, but I do believe that 'luck is what happens when preparation meets opportunity'. If I was lucky to be picked it was only because I was ready when the opportunity arose, and I was only ready because I had practised more and harder at my basic skills than anyone I knew. If only critics were able to see what effort is put in to make a good performance possible, they might be able to give credit where credit is due.

On that fateful Sunday I was completely unprepared for what was about to happen. The telephone began to ring constantly, telegrams arrived, followed over the next few days by letters from people I hadn't seen for years. Almost fifty years on I can't exactly remember who called, but I do remember one call from a gentleman called Tom Hutton. To give him his full title he was CSMI Tom Hutton, and he was a lovable animal, who helped me enormously as a player and as a man. He was an ever-present when I played Army and Combined Services rugby, and he certainly kept my feet on the ground. As a senior NCO he was heavily involved in the P Company gym and oversaw fitness for soldiers trying to pass into the Parachute Regiment. When Tom called, he asked me if I would like to come down and be introduced to his team, as he had told them a lot about me. In 1969 it was quite rare for anyone in the Armed Forces, certainly in the Army, to be capped, so I probably had some curiosity value as well.

Tuesday was the chosen day and I duly turned up at the gym at Browning Barracks, having been told to come in my kit. What I didn't know was Tom, as ever, had an ulterior motive. I was put through a workout that completely humiliated me. It was the classical sprinting in the gym between two lines, ten yards apart, touching the ground each time. I threw up pretty quickly, and whilst the onlookers didn't laugh at me, they were definitely amused at my lack of fitness.

It was all very sobering, coming at the time it did, and Tom's grinning response was that it was time I was brought down a peg or two, as I was getting a bit full of myself. He was of course absolutely right.

It was all completely unreal, with not much time to make arrangements. We made a family decision for a heavily pregnant Maureen and Robbie the dog to come to Edinburgh and stay with my parents.

We discussed driving up, but only owning a Mini, and a small matter of a rabies outbreak in the Camberley area of England, plus the fact that the SRU would pay for the rail journey, that made the train decision an easy one to make.

I found out later that had we gone by car and taken the dog, we would have been in all kinds of trouble with the authorities. Not only would Robbie have been put down, I would have been in court, possibly even court-martialled and probably fined very heavily, plus the small risk of rabies being transmitted by our pet.

On the Tuesday a letter arrived from the Scottish Rugby Union confirming my selection, hotel and travel arrangements, plus timings for the international. The SRU were not known for their generosity, so the letter which I received is reproduced next, followed by the cautionary note about expenses (see overleaf).

I hope you agree that the selection letter and expenses enclosure makes for interesting reading. The first item of note was telling me not to exchange my white jersey number 15 as it may be required for the game against France! At that time I didn't know that you had to pay for any jersey you swopped, and I certainly hadn't thought any farther ahead than this game.

There were other notable bits of penny-pinching listed in the letter: no first-class travel except under special circumstances; if your family home was in Edinburgh then the SRU were not going to allow you to stay in the North British Hotel after the match; players were expected to supply their own shorts and socks; international ties had to be purchased from R.W. Forsyth Ltd and they weren't presented by the SRU.

Readers who are accustomed to the professionalism of twenty-first century rugby will be more than a little surprised to read that the only 'private' session the team had together was on the Thursday afternoon at Murrayfield and it would only last for around two to two and a half hours.

Edinburgh,

EH12 5PJ

30th November, 1969.

Dear Sir,

Scotland v. South Africa

You have been chosen to play/~~act as reserve~~ for Scotland against South Africa at Murrayfield on Saturday 6th December, 1969. Please let me know if you are able to play/~~attend~~ by returning the attached form in the enclosed envelope after stating whether you require accommodation at the Braid Hills and/or North British Hotels. The Committee have ruled that it is unnecessary for those who reside in Edinburgh to stay at the North British Hotel on Saturday night.

Those requiring to travel from England by train overnight may do so at first class fare.

If you are doubtful as to your ability to take your place please indicate so on the form. It is imperative that I should know by not later than mid-day on Wednesday 3rd December should you subsequently become unable to play or be in any doubt whatsoever.

Arrangements

Thursday 4th December

Report at Murrayfield by 1.30 p.m. so as to be ready for training session at	2.00 p.m.
Return from Murrayfield to Braid Hills Hotel approx.	4.45 p.m.
Dinner at Braid Hills Hotel	6.30 p.m.

Friday 5th December

There will be a public practice at Myreside at	10.00 a.m. approx.
Coach departs Braid Hills Hotel	9.45 a.m.
Lunch at Braid Hills Hotel	1.00 p.m.
Tea at Hotel	4.30 p.m.
Dinner	6.30 p.m.

Saturday 6th December

Meeting at a time to be arranged by the Captain	
Lunch at Braid Hills Hotel	Time to be announced later
Transport to Murrayfield (all baggage should be taken)	– do –
White Jersey No....(5.....will be provided. This jersey should not be exchanged as it may be required for the game against France.	
Bring white shorts and plain dark blue stockings	
Team photograph	1.45 p.m.
Kick-off	2.15 p.m.
Tea at Murrayfield (in Internationalists' tearoom, stand Section 2)	
Transport to North British Hotel	5.00 p.m.
Dinner at MacRobert Pavilion, Ingliston at 7.00 p.m. for (Dress – Dinner Jacket)	7.30 p.m.
Transport leaves North British at	6.35 p.m.
2 Complimentary stand tickets are enclosed. Further tickets at 30/– can be purchased.	
Players' Room will be available at the N.B. Hotel in the evening. Each player and reserve will be issued with tickets for this room and the regulations regarding its use to be announced at the Braid Hills Hotel must be strictly adhered to.	

Scottish tie can be purchased from R W Forsyth Ltd.

Yours faithfully,

126

SCOTTISH RUGBY UNION

Instructions regarding Expenses Claims etc.

1. Where travel to Edinburgh or the venue of any "Away" match is by rail second class fare only may be charged except that those travel overnight are permitted to travel first class with sleepers in addition, provided no single berth second class sleepers are availa

2. Air travel should be at tourist rates.

3. If the length of the journey is such that a meal or meals require t be taken, the Union will bear the cost of one drink along with the cost of the said meal or meals.

4. When staying in hotels players should note that table d'hote meals only are to be taken. A la carte meals are not chargeable but one drink per meal may be charged to the Union.

5. Only the cost of bedrooms and table d'hote meals is payable by the Union. All extras such as valeting charges, telephone calls, newspapers and drinks ordered in bedrooms or hotel lounges are the responsibility of individual players and must be paid for by them.

6. Players in the International Matches may either submit their claim after each match or a full claim immediately after the Calcutta Cup Match. All claims must be submitted prior to 31st March.

7. Expenses are paid by cheque and it will greatly facilitate administration if players on receiving these cheques will cash them or pay them into their banks as soon as possible after receipt and not hold them up for several weeks as has happened in past seasons.

JOHN LAW,

Secretary, S.R.U.,
Murrayfield,
Edinburgh, EH12 5PJ.

Shortly after I found out I had been selected against the Springboks, I had a chat with John Frame, my ex-Edinburgh University centre, and a good friend, who made little attempt to improve my high state of nervousness. This was typical of John, a most unselfish player who, although he won well over twenty caps at a time where four caps a season was good going, has never got the international acclaim I believe he deserved.

He did have, and still has, a very dry sense of humour.

When asked what happened before the match, John said in no uncertain terms that the training on the Thursday afternoon at Murrayfield after we met up was absolutely knackering, and he hoped I was fit, really fit, because if I wasn't it would find me out.

He also told me about the sign above the dressing room door at Murrayfield that all the players could see as they went out. He said, just like at Wimbledon, 'If you can meet with triumph and disaster and treat these two imposters just the same.' Only at Murrayfield it says, 'If at first you don't succeed we'll find someone who can.'

I was, of course, completely taken in by all of this, and my apprehension was increased tenfold, as much of my rugby in season 1969/70 up until then had been for junior XVs at London Scottish, with Hampshire who weren't exactly a top county side, the Army and twice for Combined Services. Much of my training had been running with the dog, so I wasn't exactly full of confidence, especially after my fitness shortcomings only a couple of months earlier.

As it turned out I needn't have worried because the session was all about what we were going to do with the ball. We were able to run through the various miss-moves that John Frame and I were familiar with at university; this plus the warm greeting from everyone made me feel very much at home.

Having said that, most of the side were men I had watched, occasionally played against or never seen in my life before. Here is where professionalism has completely changed rugby. Of the Scotland XV that played the Springboks in December 1969 there were three players I had never met, and they were Peter Stagg, the giant from Sale, Ian McLauchlan from Jordanhill, and Wilson Lauder, the Scottish Welshman.

I knew Ian Robertson and had played with him twice for Edinburgh Schools and against him at university. I knew Rodger Arneil, having played against him through school. I had played against Sandy Carmichael, Frank Laidlaw, Chris Rea, Duncan Patterson, and I knew Alastair Biggar, and Sandy Hinshelwood from London Scottish, but they were in the 1st XV. I had known Gordon Brown since he was a twelve-year-old when we camped with the Scottish Schoolboys Club and had played against him once or twice. The captain was Jim Telfer. I had played against him three times and was totally in awe of him and close, in truth, to being terrified of him. The only player I had played with regularly was John Frame and we had spent three seasons in the same Edinburgh University XV.

There we were seventy-two hours before playing the Springboks, with four new caps – me, Gordon Brown, Alastair Biggar and Duncan Patterson – only the one training session behind closed doors on the Thursday afternoon, and a session for the press on the Friday. Add to this the fact that John Frame had said the Thursday session would be mainly fitness!

On the other hand, the Springboks were on tour and were training or playing six days a week. In fairness, the tour was a disaster for them from the first day, haunted by anti-apartheid demonstrators. I had lived a sheltered life, and until Peter Hain burst on to the scene I really knew nothing about conditions in South Africa.

I had played against Tommy Bedford when he was a Rhodes Scholar at Oxford, and by reputation knew about players like Jan Ellis and Piet Greyling. What I did realise was that Scotland's victories against the Springboks were as rare as hens' teeth, and that they loved testing full backs.

The Scotsman newspaper on the morning of the match wrote: 'There are many lonely places in the world but none lonelier than the square yard of turf occupied by a full back in his first international. Full backs are similar to goalkeepers in this respect and whilst Ian Smith has most of the qualities needed for an international full back, until the day we just don't know. The same held true for the goalkeeper Frank Haffey before his ignominious debut at Wembley.'

For those unfamiliar with the name Frank Haffey, he was held responsible for a 9–3 hammering by England at Wembley, and he was picked only because the top three goalkeepers in Scotland were out injured.

Every Scotsman at that time knew this tale of woe, and there was I reading the newspaper sitting up in bed in the Braid Hills Hotel, which was the base at that time of the Scottish rugby team for all their home internationals. I had the breakfast tray on my lap with bacon, egg, sausage, black pudding and tomato awaiting demolition. Suddenly my saliva dried up, and I can tell you it quite ruined my breakfast.

There is something that today's international players perhaps don't realise. It is the simple fact that they are all professionals. They will have graduated from a Premiership, Pro14, Top14 or Super Rugby side, and before that a major club's academy. They are introduced to first-team rugby at a packed Franklins Gardens, Scotstoun, La Defence Arena or similar. Not playing initially, just soaking up the atmosphere, followed by time on the bench, then on to the pitch after the first frenetic period is over. By the time they graduate to the international stage they will have experienced big crowds, television cameras, and the pace of European Cup rugby. They are also training and practising basic skills every day of the week

In the late 1960s you went from a crowd of several hundred (maximum), to tens of thousands, and millions on television. In my case, the step I took was from two men and a dog at London Scottish 3rds to the noise and atmosphere and pressure of an international. It is little wonder that not everyone survived.

As I wrote earlier, I have always been incredibly nervous before matches ever since I made a silly mistake as a small boy at school. I could play fly half, centre, wing or scrum half, with no nerves at all, but full back was just a nightmare. On this Saturday in December 1969, I knew what was to come. Piet Visagie was one of the best kicking fly halves in world rugby, and I knew the ball would be launched high into the sky early on and I simply had to catch it. That was it, bang, bust, simple, nothing else mattered. I was desperate not to let my parents down, my teammates down, and all the people who had sent me telegrams and letters. In short, I was terrified of not being good enough and looking out of my league, or to put it another way, doing a Frank Haffey.

TWELVE

Gie's us fire and fucking fury

I have often been asked what it was like to play for Scotland and winning your first cap. Although it is now forty-nine years ago there are some memories that remain quite clear. Surprisingly they are not all about the match itself; in fact, very few are.

The clearest memories are those before the match, and the first was ordering a fillet steak for lunch at the Braid Hills, prior to leaving for the ground. In those far-off days nearly everyone ate steaks before a match – no pasta, no chicken, in fact I didn't know what pasta was!

We were sitting in the dining room, I had two mouthfuls and knew I was going to be sick, so I rushed out of the dining room down a few steps into the loo, where there was a line of men standing urinating.

I pushed between two of them and threw up over their shoes. It was only then that I realised it was the selectors! The very men who had chosen me in the teeth of a lot of criticism, and I could feel their faith melting away like snow off a dyke. I crept back upstairs and ate two ice creams – no chewing and easy swallowing.

The second memory was how odd it was that, from the moment we got on the team bus to go to the ground, I suddenly felt very calm. I was nervous, but not the need to go and sit on the toilet nervous, and that is still my biggest memory. The journey to the ground was incredibly exciting with police outriders as we drove at speed through the streets of Edinburgh to Murrayfield.

The third memory was walking into the changing room and seeing my white Scotland jersey hanging up with the number fifteen on the back. Underneath it were a couple of programmes, and a pile of what seemed to be envelopes, which turned out to be a mass of good luck telegrams. Sitting reading them I realised they had come not only from the UK but all over the world. If it hadn't dawned on me before, it certainly did now, that there were a huge number of people wishing me well, and I must not let them down. They would be watching at the ground, or on television, and in some cases in countries far away listening on their radios, praying for a Scottish victory, and relying on me to do well.

My fourth memory is as we went out on to the pitch before the game, where I met George Burrell, one of the selectors, and a most lovely man. He was a sturdy Borderer, and an ex-Scotland full back himself. Standing right on the halfway line in the middle of the pitch he motioned me across. George then told me he had played at full back in the 1951 massacre of Scotland by the Springboks and, almost in tears, he said all he wanted was a win, just one point would do. That really reinforced to me how much the whole thing meant to so many people, and not just me.

Back in the 1960s the warm-up was very personal, and no one went out on to the pitch before kick-off. Instead we sneaked out behind the stand and warmed up by ourselves on the back pitch. That was weird in itself because we had to pass supporters as they streamed into the ground, and pass cars with fans picnicking and drinking, to get to the back pitch. A bit of stretching, and for me kicking and catching a few balls, then we nipped back into the changing room. I was asked to go and check the match balls as I was to be goal kicking. To be quite honest, they seemed okay to me, but unless they had been soft I wouldn't have known what the correct pressure was. This may of course explain why my kicking wasn't all it might have been!

On our return to the dressing room in the tense few minutes before running out, we were visited by the chairman of the selectors along with two henchmen. The captain asked for silence for the chairman.

'Gie's us fire and fucking fury!' he cried. That was it. He turned and left, and I don't know how the others felt, but I was gobsmacked. I suppose I'd expected some patriotic words, some encouragement, a call to the colours – not just one brief sentence.

This was followed by some running on the spot together with knees-up to the count of ten, which every team I played for seemed to do, and then a knock on the door and we were off.

I can't remember one word that Jim Telfer said, possibly because I had retreated into my own pre-match world.

I can only try to describe what that felt like, and whatever I write still feels inadequate. It was like a cross between how it would feel to have won the lottery at the same time as you became a father for the first time. Just bursting with pride, desperate to get on to the pitch, welling up with emotion as I ran out straight through the pipes and drums playing 'Scotland the Brave'.

There is no feeling like it, coming out to a wall of sound, representing your country, wearing the jersey you have coveted your entire life – the culmination of every dream that a young rugby player has . . . but it is actually happening. You aren't going to wake up and find it's Monday morning and another double maths day. Dreams do come true.

The atmosphere was odd because the police had closed both

ends of the ground. At that time Murrayfield was three standing terraces, the all-seater West Stand and a huge score box on the East Terrace opposite. You didn't need a ticket to stand on the terraces, it was just a matter of turning up on the day. The Clock End, named after the large clock that stood there, and the other end were both empty.

Despite this, Murrayfield was aggressively noisy and the game, whilst now a very distant memory, still has some totally clear moments.

I remember catching the first high ball, and the first penalty from a long way out, which I struck well and straight. I was sure it was over, but it fell agonisingly short. I'm certain that had it gone over the rest of the penalties that followed would have been different. As it was I think I missed four before my one success, which tied the match at 3–3. Piet Visagie wasn't any more successful than I was.

I didn't know until later that the reaction to my kicking failures in the family's part of the stand was not pleasant. This is where the players' nearest and dearest sit together, and apparently the crowd around them were shouting for a change of kicker, which caused my father to shout out, 'This is Ian Smith's wife. She is very pregnant, so can you please go easy!'

It must be very difficult, almost impossible, to be a family member when your loved one is having a disaster which effectively was what was happening to me. Bearing in mind the circumstances of my controversial selection I'm pretty sure the selectors weren't having a great afternoon either.

I found a letter recently while doing research for the book. It was from Major-General Forbes Finlayson, Director of the Army Dental Service. In other words, my boss, who was, by the way, a Herioter. He had written a week later congratulating me on the game but adding that halfway through the match he was getting ready to post me to Siberia.

Then everything suddenly changed . . . and my life was never to be quite the same again.

With very few minutes left to go came the moment that I had dreamed of all my life. From a lineout around the halfway line Ian Robertson called a dummy scissors move. With Chris Rea at inside centre, the ball would be passed to John Frame and I would come into the line outside John, draw the full back and put Alastair Biggar in at the corner. That was the plan taken straight from the Edinburgh University move honed to perfection between 1966 and 1968. We knew it worked perfectly when practised repeatedly, as most things do. In this situation we had practised it no more than twice, believing we all had the ability to make it work. My concern was that having found the pace of Test rugby far quicker and far more tiring than I could ever have imagined, I had serious worries about whether I had the speed to get to where I needed to be to take the pass from John.

The way I had always taken part in this move was to start deep behind the fly half and the second the scrum half had the ball I would start running across behind the two centres to straighten up outside the outside centre. If I was running at full speed as I hit the line, I should break through the defence and have only the full back to beat or to fix before passing to my winger.

It is hard, all these years later, to describe what happened next. I have of course seen it on film, but the dummy scissors worked so well that it checked H.O. de Villiers, the Springbok full back, and the field just opened up in front of me.

I could see the try line and I knew I would score even before John passed the ball. I can't articulate how it felt when I saw the space and the line beyond. To write about it now makes the hairs on the back of my neck stand up – this was a child's dream come true.

When I took the beautifully timed pass I can remember thinking I could do a one-handed touch down, but thank goodness I went for the safe option because I was tackled as I crossed the line. Here again was the difference in speed, because in club rugby it would have been an easy run-in, but I was hunted down and tackled as I scored.

The conversion attempt was a hash, as I got a touch of cramp as I got up from scoring the try. This was followed afterwards by a very stern lecture from Ian Robertson who put me very firmly – and correctly – in my place, telling me that all that mattered was for the good of Scotland, not my ego. I should have asked Jim Telfer to give the ball to Wilson Lauder instead of trying to add to my points tally.

As we were playing towards the Clock End it was impossible not to keep checking on the time and the last few minutes seemed to last forever.

But then, wonderfully, deliriously, the final whistle went and it was all over. When we made it back under the stand I was hugged by a tearful George Burrell, who had waited for eighteen years to wipe his slate clean. We had finally beaten the Springboks – for the first time in our history, dating all the way back to 1906. The significance of what we'd achieved took a long time to sink in.

On bad days when I need cheering up I can see the try on old Pathé News films on YouTube. What staggers me is how far I had to run before I got the ball. My memories are very much that I got the ball just inside the Springboks' twenty-five-yard line, but the film shows it was not far beyond the ten-yard line. When you add where I started from, which must have been behind Ian Robertson, I well inside our own half, so it's no wonder I was tired!

Looking back, I think I was in shock and had no idea of the importance of the match in the context of the Springbok tour, the anti-apartheid demonstrations, and what a pivotal moment we were all part of. It was only arriving in the North British hotel bedroom to change into black tie for the dinner when I saw the BBC news on the television. The headline story was my try, which was on a large screen behind the late Richard Baker. I suddenly realised the international we'd just taken part in was dwarfed in its importance by the sheer scale of the anti-apartheid demonstrations, and why they were taking place.

The press coverage was obviously extensive, and over the years I have occasionally looked back over the cuttings I kept. What follows is the one press report that meant more to me than any other. It was written by Vivian Jenkins, the famous Welsh full back, in the *Sunday Times* and it still sets my heart pounding to have this written by such a man.

'Ian Smith is Scotland's Rugby Hero'

Ian Smith, a name famous in Scottish rugby history, was resounding around Edinburgh again last night. Long years ago, in the '20's and early '30's, the great Scottish winger of that name, 32 times capped and nicknamed 'The Flying Scotsman', was scoring tries galore for his country with high-kneed pounding running. But the Ian Smith who thrilled 40,000 of his countrymen yesterday was a 25-year old newcomer, and Army Dental captain from Aldershot, playing in his first international match, and the try he scored that enabled his side to beat the mighty Springboks by a penalty goal and a try to a penalty goal will be talked of for as long as the many recorded by his illustrious predecessor. It came in the 31st minute of the second half, when the scores were level at a penalty goal apiece, and the game, which had not been a great one, looked like fizzling out into an undistinguished draw.

Scotland suddenly roused themselves for a last desperate effort and took play down to the Springbok's 25, far out to the left from the posts. There a scrum was ordered, and Scotland won the ball for Paterson, who made a praiseworthy debut at scrum half, to send away his partner, Ian Robertson, with a well-timed pass. Robertson veered slightly right, and with the centre Rea cutting inwards as if to take a short pass, the fly half missed him out altogether, and sent out a long pass to Frame at second centre. Frame, all 14-stone of him, then made a searing burst through the middle and then, wonder of wonders, Smith, coming up at astonishing pace from full back, was there to take an outside pass from Frame with the line staring at him about 15 yards ahead.

Two Springbok defenders coming across tried all they knew to cut Smith off, but he put back his head and went for the line as though the whole future of Scotland depended upon it, and to a thunderclap of cheering, he won the race to score. Earlier, just after half time, it was he who had kicked Scotland's penalty goal from 35 yards out to cancel out Visagie's similar effort just before half time, which had given the touring team a 3-0 lead at the interval.

Thus Smith was responsible for all of Scotland's points, even though for a long time it looked as he was going to be the villain of the piece instead of, as it actually turned out, the hero. In the first half he had missed with four attempts at penalty goals, from 52, 35, and 40 yards, and when he came up just after half time to make his fifth attempt people were saying all round me that Telfer as captain should have given the kick to someone else. But this time Smith, a left footed kicker, was on the mark and when he scored his match-winning try at the end, all of course, was forgiven.

Nor did people mind he failed with the conversion attempt after his own try. The remarkable thing about him is that he has been almost unheard of in the top circle until these last few weeks. While playing for London Scottish, he has been unable to win a first team place, owing to the presence of two other Scottish internationalists, Stewart Wilson and Gordon MacDonald, in the full back position. It is only through playing for the Army and Combined Services that he has been able to push his way to the front, and even then he would probably not have played in this match against the Springboks if another product of his old school, George Heriot's, in the person of Colin Blaikie had he been fit.

Heriot's have a remarkable tradition of producing full backs for Scotland and Smith is the seventh in line in succession to such names as DS Drysdale, JM Kerr, T Gray, IHM Thomson, Ken Scotland, and Blaikie.

Nor did he let his old school down, because apart from the missed kicks he played a thoroughly good game in other respects. His punting particularly with his left foot was particularly long.

Finally on the subject of the Springboks match was the following quote in *The Scotsman*:

Frame blazed through, all fourteen stones and more. And then, as Smith appeared outside him, gave to the full back exactly as he used to do so often in their student days, Smith scoring without recourse to Biggar on the wing.

No better try ever lit Murrayfield, and in the scoring of it, Smith's pace and acceleration into the line surprised more than just the Springboks.

'It was,' said Tommy Bedford the Springboks captain, 'the kind of try you get from short tours and national squads – no virtually scratch XV have much chance of scoring that kind of try against Test class opposition . . .

The two things that can be extracted from this quote, are '*exactly as he used to do so often in their student days*' and '*no virtually scratch XV have much chance of scoring that kind of try against test class opposition*'.

It has been written about in this story before, but the work done by the University team in '66, '67, and '68 paid huge dividends here. Because there was only television coverage of international matches at that time, unlike the blanket screening of rugby today, it would have been impossible for any international side arriving from abroad to have any idea about the miss-moves developed in Edinburgh, that were about to be used against them.

There was a window of opportunity here which remained open for about another fourteen months at the most, to use these moves before a strategy was put in place to counter them.

THIRTEEN

If they could take international caps away

In fairness I didn't play particularly well in the weeks following my first international cap. It would be not a lie to say it was probably the worst sequence of games in my life, which culminated in a pretty poor trial match at Murrayfield when the Possibles beat the Probables pretty easily 29–19, and I was in the Probables!

The match report didn't make for very good reading.

For full back Ian Smith it was not a particularly happy occasion. Missed tackles and misjudged line kicks adding to his goal kicking failures must have left the selectors wishing for a miraculous return to fitness of former cap Colin Blaikie.

With so few alternatives for the position, one can only hope that Smith, like most of his team-mates, can put much of their trial form behind them for a week on Saturday.

For the match against France, the selectors fortunately kept faith with the side, with the exception of Gordon Connell coming in for the unfit Duncan Patterson. As we gathered in a snowbound Edinburgh, we had to train on the Thursday in a gym, and I can well remember snow piled at the side of the pitch at Murrayfield. There had been an electric blanket installed in 1959 which meant that the pitch was always playable even after heavy frosts, which were a frequent occurrence.

Prior to this, wintry conditions posed a constant threat to matches and attempts to protect the playing surface consisted of tent-like canopies with tall paraffin heaters within, being pitched over the playing area – supplemented by tons of straw. The remarkable thing about these rather Heath Robinson-like arrangements was that they did work, and I remember throughout my childhood seeing the pitch with flecks of straw. In 1963 in Paris, prior to the France versus Scotland match at Colombes Stadium the pitch was frozen and the French authorities set it on fire to make the surface playable!

As we came out on that cold January day in 1970 the chill was incredible, and I was a great deal more nervous than I had been for the Springboks match, because Colin Blaikie was almost fit again, and I just had to find some form. Fortunately for me, when their fly half, Lucien Paries, launched his first kick of the match, it was a long diagonal and I was able to catch it running left and got in a decent kick away which settled my nerves a great deal.

To score a try in my first international was a dream come true, and I never for one second thought it would happen again. But then we set up an attack again, Ian Robertson this time calling an Edinburgh University 'miss two' move with John Frame at inside centre passing left and missing out Chris Rea to spin the ball straight to me. Chris's running line fixed the French midfield defence and I was able to hit a huge hole in the line between Alain Marot at outside centre and Roger Bourgarel on the wing, crossing the score without any French defenders even getting close to me. On reflection it seemed strange that in two consecutive internationals no one seemed to know how to counter these simple back moves. I was almost thinking this international stuff was all too easy.

We were well beaten by France in the end and I was on the wrong end of a tackle that saw Benoit Dauga, the massive French number eight, pick up a few yards from our line and just run straight at me. He was so big I swear that he blotted out the sun. Although I hit him with all I had, there is a photo somewhere of him leaning his elbow on the ground, his hand on his chin, while the other hand gently touched the ball down to score and I'm sprawled on my back, hanging on to his ankles.

Distance does make the memory fade, and for years I was certain that Dauga had picked up from a scrum and Ian Robertson had gone missing, but subsequent views of old Pathé news film showed that was a real insult to a great fly half.

The legendary Bill McLaren had his own take on the Dauga try: 'Lesser mortals faced with a Dauga breathing fire might have sought refuge behind the clock.'

The match report by Norman Mair in *The Scotsman* made for very interesting reading. '*Ian Smith, in scoring his own and Scotland's second try of the season in only his second international, almost certainly achieved something which, for a full back, is without parallel in almost a century of international rugby.*'

Until that moment it hadn't crossed my mind that the two tries I had scored were the exception and not the rule. I just assumed that wonderful attacking full backs like Ken Scotland had scored international tries. In 1988 I was given a present of *The Phoenix Book of International Rugby Records* by John Griffiths covering 1871–1987, and I found that I was the first Scottish full back in history to have scored a try in Test rugby.

However, it didn't take me long to realise that certain newspaper correspondents in England were not much taken by me, specifically John Reason of the *Daily Telegraph* and Robin Marlar in the *Sunday Times*.

Reason was always a very good judge of a rugby player, and the fact he wasn't my number one fan probably shows how right he was!

Marlar, on the other hand, was a very good cricketer, and he certainly insulted a few decent players, sometimes to his own detriment. I suffered at his hands not long after my first cap. I think it was the Saturday before Scotland played France in 1970 and I was playing for the Army against Harlequins at Twickenham. In those far-off days the only Saturday match an international was encouraged to miss, and indeed expected not to play, was before his first cap. After that you turned out for your club side as normal. We were awful and were beaten by a big margin, and I faced Harlequin after Harlequin coming through the middle running at me and I didn't make too many effective tackles, although there were some mitigating factors in this – I was desperate to play the following week against France as I was determined not to be a one-cap wonder. Thus I wasn't at all keen to injure myself, which isn't very good really, but I hope understandable.

As I sat on the Sunday morning eating my bacon and eggs, toast and marmalade and scanning the *Sunday Times* I came upon Marlar's match report. It will come as no surprise to know it wasn't one I kept, but the gist of it was as follows.

Ian Smith stood like a traffic policeman waving past the Harlequins three-quarters. If they could take international caps away they should take his. He was never an international quality full back and should never have been selected in the first place.

Everyone is of course entitled to their opinion, but I can tell you it did spoil my breakfast and, as I was to discover later, I wasn't the only one to suffer from his opinions.

I don't quite know what I expected when all the fuss died down after the insane excitement of the match against the Springboks, but I certainly discovered life as a current internationalist did not prove very easy.

I received a phone call not long after the Springbok match from London Scottish, and the gist of the conversation was that I would now be the 1st XV full back. This was the beginning of a difficult few months, as the reason for the call became clear.

'It is club policy that current internationals play for the firsts.'

This had provided the club with an interesting problem because Gordon Macdonald, who had opposed me when Combined Services played Scottish Districts, was not only the 1st XV captain but also the very well-established and highly thought of full back.

The poor man, who had a very short international career of about three minutes as an early replacement against Ireland in 1969, deserved better than having an off day when I had one of the best days of my life, culminating in my first cap. What happened was that London Scottish were to play him at fly half to accommodate me at full back, knowing full well I would be absent playing for Scotland and quite frequently the Army. Life at the Richmond Athletic Ground was quite tricky in that Gordon didn't really utter one word to me for the remainder of that season, not in the changing room during a team talk, on the pitch or at training.

As a consequence I never really felt I belonged at Scottish because understandably Gordon was very popular, an excellent full back and he had been replaced by an upstart who had come into the club and taken his place. Added to this, they didn't think I was much good either.

In sober and mature reflection, I really can't – and don't – blame him at all. If the boot had been on the other foot I'm not certain I could have let the season go by without several unpleasant and caustic remarks, and to his eternal credit that never happened.

Any mistakes I made were not quite applauded but were the subject of pointed discussion around me (if not to me) in the bar afterwards. If I had done something well I never quite felt appreciated by the supporters. To be fair, for a few months that didn't happen very often.

Having said all that about playing at London Scottish, there were good times, some great matches and a couple of entertaining moments worth relating. One of the funniest things that happened was the permanent struggle to keep two of our consistently best players away from a Scotland selector by the name of George Thomson.

His brief was obviously to watch Scottish players in England, which made him quite a frequent visitor to London Scottish. I don't know how the others felt but I was always in a position of slight trepidation when the word came that George was in the stand. He was, I eventually found out, eminently fair and, as I discovered much later, a very brave man who won the Distinguished Service Cross on Arctic convoys during the war. A future president of the SRU, he was amongst the first to realise that coaching was the way forward and he was very much a man ahead of his time. How I wish we knew more of his history earlier and not after it was too late, because we never gave him the respect he deserved.

George told me at one point that the selectors were going to travel down to London Scottish en masse on the Saturday after the Scotland Districts versus Combined Services match to see me play for Scottish Extra A to confirm that my performance had not been a fluke. Thankfully the match was cancelled!

I should explain here that if you moved to England from Scotland and wanted to play for Scotland it was almost necessary to play for London Scottish, because if the selectors ever came south then it was to the Athletic Ground at Richmond. The problem with George coming to London Scottish concerned two players of tremendous ability. Firstly, there was Alastair McHarg who won forty-four caps as a brilliant second row. He and Peter Brown were both slightly built, both outstanding footballers, great handlers of a ball, and incredibly mobile; something not usually found in second row forwards of my vintage. Indeed, I have been in the situation where the ball was kicked over my head, and as I turned to chase it, I nearly ran into Ali and Peter. For me the worst thing of all was the fact that their clearance kicks were invariably better than mine would have been.

One press correspondent always stated that when Peter and Ali played together in the second row that Scotland had a 'back five' as opposed to a 'front five', which was definitely a tribute to their mobility and lack of ballast.

Secondly, there was Gordon 'GC' Connell, one of the best scrum halves I played with or against. He and I played for Edinburgh Schools, and I watched his debut for Scotland against England in 1968 when he dropped a goal, virtually lying on his back under the posts. He had a pass every bit as long as Gareth Edwards and had one of the briefest of brief Lions careers in the amateur era. If I remember rightly he was summonsed in the last week of the 1968 tour of South Africa, played in the last three matches, but couldn't keep or swop his Test jersey because Gareth Edwards and Roger Young had been promised them already!

I digress, because the biggest problem was when George came to run his eye over London Scottish he could always be found in the bar afterwards and both Alastair and GC, with a couple of beers inside them, would go and find him and pick a verbal fight. This was not calculated to improve their chances of selection, especially with Alastair competing with Peter Brown, Peter Stagg and Gordon Brown, whilst GC was up against Ian 'Spivvy' McCrae, Duncan Paterson and Graham Young.

It was like a game, with players getting between an increasingly verbose couple and George, but sadly not always succeeding.

The try against the Springboks in 1969.

After the try – notice the empty terrace behind due to the apartheid protests.

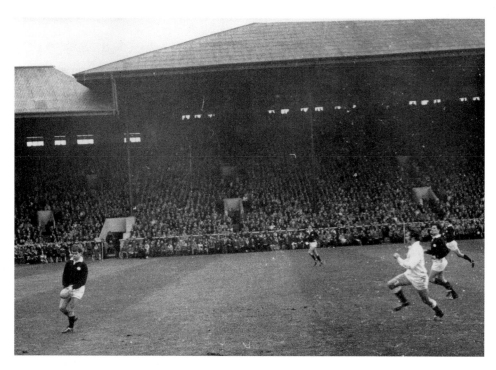

Will he or won't he kick with his right foot vs England Murrayfield 1970 . . .?

He goes for the left foot!

England 1970, Ian Robertson (with hair) and Ali Biggar. Tackled player is John Novak, who I think was also a dentist! I can just hear Donald Hastie: 'Smith, get your head on the right side!'

Scotland vs new South Wales in Australia. Once again put into space by John Frame, but ball tucked under one arm!

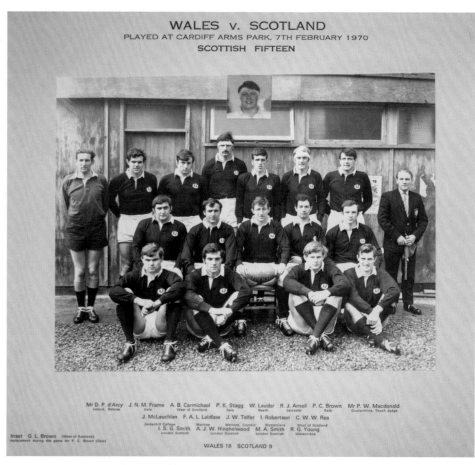

WALES v. SCOTLAND
PLAYED AT CARDIFF ARMS PARK, 7TH FEBRUARY 1970
SCOTTISH FIFTEEN

Mr D. P. d'Arcy   J. N. M. Frame   A. B. Carmichael   P. K. Stagg   W. Lauder   R. J. Arneil   P. C. Brown   Mr P. W. Macdonald
Ireland, Referee   Gala   West of Scotland   Sale   Neath   Leicester   Gala   Dunfermline, Touch Judge

J. McLauchlan   F. A. L. Laidlaw   J. W. Telfer   I. Robertson   C. W. W. Rea
Jordanhill College   Melrose   Melrose, Captain   Watsonians   West of Scotland

I. S. G. Smith   A. J. W. Hinshelwood   M. A. Smith   R. G. Young
London Scottish   London Scottish   London Scottish   Watsonians

Inset   G. L. Brown   (West of Scotland)
replacement during the game for P. C. Brown (Gala)

WALES 18   SCOTLAND 9

The official team photo before playing Wales in Cardiff in 1971.

Miss-one move going through the gap outside John Dawes, the future 1971 Lion's captain, on 7th February 1970 at a packed Cardiff Arms Park. Note ball in two hands!

This was taken during the Friday run out before Ireland 1971 – which proved to be my last cap. Following this match, my next game was for the London Scottish 2nd XV!

A very proud London Scottish 1st XV player.

A very proud moment, captaining the Irish Guards to the Land Forces Cup in Hong Kong 1972. I'm fourth right in the front row. Alastair Biggar, the 1971 Lion, is fourth rigth in the back row.

Hong Kong XV for the Asian Games, 1972. I'm the player on the right holding the ball.

1st Battalion King's Rugby squad, 1972/73.

Hong Kong vs Japan 1974 – my last international. I have four caps for Hong Kong, two against Japan, and Thailand, and Korea. In this picture, I'm the last blue jersey on the right-hand side of the front row.

Heriot's F. P. - Hong Kong VII
27th March, 1974

J. D. Sykes 1950–58   P. W. Wight 1949–59   K. J. Rowbottom 1959–65   R. Marrian 1961–65   I. Young 1947–60
D. A. H. Hardy 1952–59   C. H. Wilken   (Elgin Academy)   I. S. G. Smith 1949–63

UNION PHOTO STUDIO
TEL: H- 228715

The Heriot's FP Hong Kong VII, 1974.

Family Christmas 2017 .

FOURTEEN

I believe you are playing for Scotland against Wales this afternoon. Well, your wife has just had a son

From April 1969 and then throughout seasons 1969/70 and 1970/71, my life changed completely. Instead of being single and responsible only to myself I now had a wife, Maureen, who spent much of that time either pregnant or, after February 1970, with a small son.

As a young married army officer, I didn't qualify for an army quarter, but was accommodated in a cottage out in the country – which wasn't on a bus route. In fact, the nearest building was a pub about six hundred yards away. There were no shops to walk to, and I was away playing rugby twice a week, plus international weekends, and overnights with the Army and Combined Services XVs.

We had a Mini Traveller, which didn't work very well in the wet. It had rust holes in the floor where we could see the road rushing by, there being no MOT in those days because the vehicle was less than ten years old.

I had exchanged a decent left-hand drive Mercedes for this Mini Traveller on my return from Germany and the salesman must have seen me coming a mile off. My poor wife was stranded with either a car which took some starting, made more difficult because it was parked on grass some fifty yards off the road, or I had the car. It must have been a miserable time for her and very lonely. I feel very guilty now, but your thought processes are different when you are chasing a dream. Although it is a pretty pathetic excuse.

How different life was then, because in the beginning we had no television, washing machine, dishwasher or freezer. There were no mobile phones, or computers, or social media, just the radio for company. When I look back I just don't know how Maureen survived those two long rugby seasons, which included a Scotland tour to Australia in May 1970, when I left her with a three-month-old son.

I must leave it up to the reader to decide whether I was plain selfish in the pursuit of my dream or just a bad husband and father.

As part of any judgement there must be the match against Wales at Cardiff Arms Park. Thus far I had only worn a white jersey for Scotland, as both our games had been at home, and we changed jerseys to avoid a colour clash. Our next game was to be Wales at Cardiff Arms Park on 7 February 1970, and my first time in the blue jersey. It was to be a day I'll never forget. Maureen was heavily pregnant and due at any time. Should I have called off because of the imminent arrival of my first child? Undoubtedly there were a nervous few days before the game, because of the chance that the baby would be born. We decided that when I went to Wales, Maureen would move in with the Molloys. Mick Molloy was the Irish second row with Willie John McBride, as well as being an army doctor, so we played together for the Royal Army Medical Corps. It therefore wasn't unreasonable for me to go to Wales as Maureen had round-the-clock company, with the bonus of Mick being a doctor. That has always been my argument, based entirely on my selfishness because I had never worn the blue jersey, and had always wanted to play at Cardiff Arms Park more than anywhere else. The most compelling and utterly selfish reason was that if I called off then Colin Blaikie would probably have come in, and as I felt he was a better player than I was, then I might never get picked again.

On the morning of the match I was having my breakfast when I was asked to go to the phone.

The voice on the other end said, 'I believe you are playing for Scotland against Wales this afternoon. Well, your wife has just had a son.'

I had become the proud father of a son, Simon McGregor Gibson Smith, which made a special day even more special.

This meant the unbelievable thrill of being a father for the first time, plus wearing the blue jersey for the first time, meant that I broke down in tears during the singing of 'Land of My Fathers'. Thankfully in those far-off days you didn't line up in front of the stand, instead you would be running around keeping loose when the band struck up the anthems, so you just stood perfectly still to attention wherever you were. I was facing a part of the ground that was under construction so wasn't looking at anyone as I sobbed my heart out. It could have been a little tricky to explain!

The unanswered question remains. Should I have gone back to Aldershot to be with my wife and newborn son?

The answer is I'm still not sure. What I do know is Maureen went into labour on the Friday evening, and I don't know whether or not she didn't want me called, and sadly she has now passed away, so I can't ask her.

The other side of that particular coin is the fact that had I left on the Friday evening or Saturday morning there was no ready full back replacement available, so I would have been letting Scotland and our supporters down.

Even allowing for the distraction of the possibility of Maureen having the baby in my absence, I was more than a little tense before the Welsh match for two reasons.

The first was an idiotic interview I had given which appeared as an article with a photograph in the *Radio Times*. In the sixties and seventies if you wanted to know in advance what was on the very small number of television channels and radio channels you bought the weekly *Radio Times*. It had a pretty big circulation, and when they rang me up and asked if they could write a short article about me I was really surprised and with no hesitation agreed. Little did I know what was to appear after they came to the house, talked to us both, and took some photographs of me in army uniform.

When I saw the article, I couldn't believe my eyes. It was headlined 'The Other Ian Smith Warns Wales'. A photograph showed me in my uniform holding a rugby ball in front of a gorse bush and looking like a complete prat.

This was around the time that Ian Smith, who was the prime minister of Southern Rhodesia, had declared unilateral independence after a minority white electorate had voted in favour of this plan of action. He was therefore headline news in the papers and on television. The *Radio Times* article about me went on to say I practised my goal kicking over gorse bushes outside my house. With my goal kicking record, you can imagine how much the rip was taken out of me when the team assembled.

Secondly, the forecast was for strong winds, one of my great fears, and that was of course what happened. The wind was blowing almost straight down the pitch, and I discovered we were playing with it in the first half, and how I hated that.

There were two off-the-field incidents that I knew nothing about until later. The first concerned Peter Stagg, who found a large hole in his blue socks and couldn't persuade the SRU to stump up for a replacement pair, so he had to coat his leg in black shoe polish. This was fairly typical of the meanness of the SRU, who wouldn't allow me to spend Saturday night in the North British Hotel in Edinburgh after home matches because my parents lived in the city. The same SRU who included a sentence in your selection letter demanding that you bring the jersey you wore in your last match otherwise there would be a charge for a replacement – something that I put to the test . . . and was duly billed for!

I have never forgotten being told by Colonel Charles Usher, who played for Scotland before the First World War, was next capped in the first international after the Armistice, against France at Parc des Princes on the 1 January 1920, and the SRU told him to wear the jersey he wore in his last match!

Rodger Arneil took this to heart and washed his jersey but the colour ran through the white thistle and he had to have a new one anyway!

The second incident was that Mike Smith, who was winning his first cap on the wing, announced that as a doctor he had diagnosed himself with appendicitis, and he couldn't possibly play. Apparently he only arrived on the pitch after the anthems, and the selectors had convinced him that all he had was an attack of acute nervousness!

At Cardiff I have few memories but one that was quite clear was a miss-one move from John Frame which put me into space outside John Dawes, then running up to J.P.R. Williams at full back with Mike Smith outside me. I saw JPR turn towards Mike, so far I almost saw both shoulders. I should have pinned my ears back and gone for the line myself, but I passed to Mike instead. He looked at me, looked at JPR, and dropped the ball. I'm sure it was my pass!

How lucky we were to be using the miss-move with my Edinburgh University friend John Frame in my first three internationals and get away with it. This wouldn't happen today because everything is under the analysts' view on a bank of computers. Every new move is studied in detail and anything that looks remotely different is scrutinised again and again in slow motion to ensure defensive counters are put in place.

When you think that every Premiership, Pro14, Top14 and Super Rugby game is televised, so there is no escape from any aspect of the game, be it punches thrown, tackling without the use of arms, or a new move. Pundits on channels like Sky and BT Sport use slow motion replays to look in detail at what teams and individuals are doing to break down defences.

The second half started with a lineout inside the Welsh twenty-five and Gareth Edwards hoisted a high kick which, as I feared, was still rising as it passed over my head as the wind swirled into our faces. I scrambled back and gathered it inside our twenty-five in the middle of the pitch. Strangely when I got my hands on it I noticed that the wind appeared to have shifted and I was able to get a decent kick in down the opposite touchline. I learned later that this was due to the swirl of the wind which is a common feature in most international grounds because of the large stands and open ends of the grounds. Apparently it makes goal kicking a lot more difficult – which became a very handy excuse for my awful kicking performance against the Springboks, because I could also say it affected Piet Visagie as well!

The match in Cardiff was another example of how fickle selectors were. They had plucked Graham Young, a good club scrum half at Watsonians, out of the blue to partner Ian Robertson, also a Watsonian. Although he didn't do much wrong, they never picked Graham again. I still cannot understand how selectors can think you are good enough one week and not the next.

The dinner after the match was a great affair, I was celebrating the birth of my son, very much encouraged by John Dawes who I was lucky enough to be sitting next to. I think I probably lost three or four hours of my life that night, and I'm not sure where they went. It's only later I realised how lucky I'd been to have the company of a future Lions captain for an evening whose sole aim was to get me drunk – and he succeeded very well indeed.

There was one press cutting that I have kept that related to that match and the difficulty I had persuading the English press I was any good!

One can imagine such attack minded full backs as our own Ian Smith revelling in the firm going and fluid exchanges expected in Australia. Not that the same Smith neglects his defensive duties when the day demands. Such as at the Arms Park where he celebrated his first ever match on that dread pitch with an immaculate display of fielding and kicking against the gale in the first half.

So much for a certain English critic who loftily opined with doubtless a touch of sour grapes at Smith's feat in scoring a try in each of his first two internationals, that "the myth of Smith would be exploded in Cardiff".

Dublin came next, and another defeat. It was to prove to be Jim Telfer's swansong, although no one realised it at the time.

I had been told to stay out of the line because I 'slowed everyone down', so my secret was out. It had finally been confirmed that I really was a full back slower than your average prop.

The amateur nature of everything surrounding international rugby was best described on the Thursday lunchtime before the Irish match when we arrived in the dining room of the Shelbourne Hotel in Dublin for lunch.

As the Scottish team (plus selectors) walked in we were confronted by the entire Irish team already seated. What happened next was our selectors telling us to leave, and the entire Irish team standing up inviting us to take a seat. We ended up having lunch together before they were moved out, and you cannot imagine that happening today.

I don't have too many memories of the game, apart from the fact I dropped my first catch, not something to inspire my teammates, and then my friend Mick Molloy barged over the top of me to score a try. To add insult to injury, he rubbed my hair as he got up and asked how Maureen was!

I can also remember facing what seemed like five laughing Irishmen all in a huge overlap, who passed it from one to the other and there was absolutely nothing I could do about it. The highlight of the match was Mike Smith's try. I saw it from the ground having come into the line and had to simply guide the ball on with my left hand, as I didn't have time to catch and pass before I was flattened.

After the game, there was tea in the Lansdowne clubhouse, and a big queue at the bar. John Frame said we might get a drink at the other end of the stand in the Dublin Wanderers clubhouse, where we met Kevin Flynn and Kevin Kelly with whom I had played in a game at West Hartlepool. Five pints later we left in a hurry to get to the dinner, me on an almost empty stomach, and rushing in late we found Peter Stagg lining up a row of whiskeys, which he proceeded to solemnly drink one after the other.

I don't know whether the rumour about Peter was true, which was that he refused to be measured so no one ever knew how tall he was. He was certainly the tallest player I have ever been on a rugby pitch with. The rumour was that on the 1968 Lions tour, Peter was asleep on a beach in South Africa and John Reason of the *Daily Telegraph* placed a sandshoe opposite Peter's head, and another opposite his feet, and from that he claimed to have measured Peter at seven feet!

I was to run into Peter outside a tube station in London in the 1980s when the sun was suddenly blotted out, and there he was. I said to him that he hadn't changed much, and his response was neither had I and that I was still small and fat!

FIFTEEN

Ian Smith has never been tested under the high ball and Shackleton the England fly half will certainly test him on Saturday

When the side to play England was announced, Jim Telfer had gone and I couldn't believe it. The man was, and remains, a legend, and that he could be dismissed so summarily was a real shock. With one match of the season to go, admittedly followed by a game against the Barbarians, followed by a tour to Australia, perhaps one more game and then a clean break might have been fairer.

Frank Laidlaw, our hooker, was appointed as captain, and what a lovely man he was. On the morning of our match against Wales, knowing my son Simon had just been born, he spent breakfast using table napkins to show me how to do a nappy!

On the Thursday afternoon when we all gathered in the dressing room at Murrayfield, Frank began his captaincy by announcing he wanted Stagg to stand at one or two in the lineout with his arms in the air on England's throw. Bearing in mind that it was the wingers who threw in to the lineout, and at that time there was no lifting, every lineout was a bunfight anyway and Frank's idea was pure genius. Peter Stagg at seven feet or thereabouts with his arms in the air made accurate throwing almost impossible. Remember, wings had better things to do than practise throwing in, so the accuracy was almost non-existent, and England's much-vaunted second row won almost no ball at all.

It was the Wednesday evening before the match that began the worst three days of my international career. At that time there was a programme on BBC television called *Sportsnight with Coleman* and this particular evening they decided to focus on the 'up-and-under' as an attacking weapon, with films of J.P.R. Williams being smashed under a high ball. My predecessor, Colin Blaikie, was shown having a high ball bounce off his chest and scooped up by David Duckham who promptly scored, plus several other incidents which highlighted how lethal a high ball could be if properly executed.

This brief interlude finished with the comment, 'Ian Smith has never been tested under the high ball and Shackleton the England fly half will certainly test him on Saturday.' All I can remember was going almost straight away to the loo and being sick. I hated high balls, or up-and-unders, although I had a good record of catching them – but this was something different. If anyone reading this sentence has any experience of this kind of pressure, they will understand.

I didn't sleep properly on the three nights that followed, with recurring nightmares of dropping the ball or knocking it on, then England scoring because of my failure. This was not helped by the following article by Bill McLaren in a national newspaper, read no doubt by the England team as well:

England profit from adroit use of Garryowen

An immediate red alert for an English Garryowen would seem to be of priority importance in Scotland's plans to regain the Calcutta Cup at Murrayfield on Saturday. Recent evidence bears out that England more than most have made life hazardous for full backs and profitable for themselves by adroit use of the up-and-under carrying the requisite amount of 'up'.

Remember how at Twickenham a year ago John Finlan did some saturation bombing of Scotland's full back Colin Blaikie, from one of whose errors David Duckham snatched a ricochet to score the first of his two tries that won the match? This season, two of England's five tries have stemmed from high punts by their fly half Roger Shackleton. The one against Ireland enabled his Cambridge University colleague, John Spencer, to flatten Tom Kiernan for Shackleton's try and in the Welsh match it was the full back again John Williams this time who was clobbered by John Novak for a brilliant try by Duckham.

Big three-quarters

The point is that currently England possess the right kind of equipment to make maximum impact in more ways than one. Given room to use his stronger left boot, Shackleton can hoist a ball and make it hover as Novak, Duckham, and Spencer take off towards the landing area like wild rhinos. And those exert considerable psychological influence in that each is extremely well fed and combative.

Indeed, the English threequarter line averages out at 14st 2lb and just over 6ft 1in and are surprisingly quick on the hoof. It is one thing to stand fast in the face of advancing pigmies; another, in the matter of resolve, as seven hundredweights of prime English three-quarter beef approaches.

So when the siren sounds, whoever is to be Scotland's hero of the moment must signal loud and clear, mutter a brief prayer – he should be facing in the appropriate direction for that anyway – and hope that planning had ensured support both around and behind.

Fortunately for Scotland, not only is their full back, Ian Smith, a young man of admirable courage, but his well-nourished frame, solid to the ground, is not easily uprooted.

This article didn't make me feel any better, indeed if anything it made me feel worse.

I always enjoyed my breakfast in bed on the morning of the match, but inevitably that went as well. Ice cream was my salvation, but the disappearance of tension on the team bus didn't happen either.

However, reading this in 2019 and thinking about some of the massive centres playing international rugby these days, the English centres of the 1970 vintage are puny by comparison!

If we look at a small selection of international three-quarters plying their trade in 2019, Mathieu Bastareaud at 6ft and 18st 13lbs is one case in point, George North 6ft 4in and around 17st, and Manu Tuilangi at 6ft 1in and 17st 5lb. Am I happy I'm not playing today? Yes!

To return to the high ball and the Calcutta Cup match, I think England kicked off, and there was a lineout to the left of the posts, with Scotland's backs to the Clock End, just about on the ten-yard line, and an England throw-in. The entire English back division grinned at me, and with their hands held palm upwards and moving them up and down made no bones about what was going to happen! Happily, Frank Laidlaw's cunning lineout plan worked, and we spoilt their ball. A scrum was the result, with England's put-in and the same gestures happened all over again.

This seemed to go on for an eternity but, in reality, it was probably only a few minutes before Shackleton got his high kick away. I remember it all very clearly, as I knew our posts were behind me to the right, I was inside our twenty-five, and my onboard computer told me that this was going to need to be a definite mark, and the English backs were going to be on top of me.

Turning left to catch it, so a dropped ball wouldn't be knocked on, I deliberately fell as I screamed for a mark and I was conscious of being at the same time – but I knew I had made the catch, and the whistle told me I had been successful.

The relief was unbelievable, and I was so pleased with myself, the touch-kick was right-footed as well, and it actually screw-kicked to touch! As far as I remember there were no other high balls to deal with.

I do feel this jumping for the ball, as is the way things are in rugby today, is a mistake. The number of yellow and red cards issued and, more importantly, the number of injuries is far too high. If calling for a mark was allowed anywhere on the pitch once again, there would be far less aimless kicking, fewer cards and a reduction in injuries. Add to that the lineout following a touch-kick from the mark would be awarded to the kicker's team and this would probably almost eliminate aimless kicking upfield. I also believe it takes more courage to stand your ground than jump in the air, because in theory no one can touch you while you are airborne whilst standing still you know what is coming. I have always thought the up-and-under aimed at the posts with a full back trapped, is one of the scariest things on a rugby pitch.

My only other memory of the match was being beaten all ends up by John Spencer, which was annoying because I always prided myself on not being beaten on the outside, but he beat me easily, to score a really great seventy-yard try. To be fair, there was no touchline to help as we were in the middle of the pitch, and he was a world-class centre, and I am slower than your average prop, but it still rankles all these years on!

So the Calcutta Cup was won by Scotland, 14–5. At the time I had no idea how infrequently Scottish players were to be able to say that. Gregor Townsend, a great player and now a formidable coach, apparently only beat England once in ten attempts. I'm always pleased to be able to tell my English friends that I only played England once and my record is played one, won one!

After the post-match dinner, when we were at home in Edinburgh, there was always a players' room in the North

British Hotel, which was either the epicentre of enjoyment, and unlimited champagne, or a place of desolation where the drink was very much more limited. After we beat England in 1970, the English players were in the room as well, and I knew Nigel Starmer-Smith better than most of their players, having played against him as a student when Oxford University played Edinburgh University. Then we played club rugby, county rugby, and I also played against him for the Army versus Harlequins. It came as a shock to find he was distinctly unfriendly, even abusive. I put this down to disappointment, and it was to be another year before I, to my cost, found out why.

The tale is simply one of revenge being a dish best served cold. Nigel and I were playing for the Camberley Presidents XV against Camberley (to celebrate an opening of something which I now can't remember). We threw in to a lineout five yards from our line, and I indicated I'd take the pass standing near the dead-ball line and clear. That was okay until the pass, which was thrown in the air like an up-and-under followed by a bellowed, 'Call me Spermers, you bastard!'

Nigel laughed himself silly as I got smashed by most of the Camberley pack, and then afterwards I discovered what it was all about.

Apparently when Oxford University came to Craiglockhart in the mid 1960s and I was secretary of the university rugby club there was a misprint in the programme, with the Oxford scrum half listed as N. Spermer-Smith. I did remember Nigel sitting with a pile of paper scribbling away like mad before the match, and to this day I still have one of the altered programmes.

As I was secretary he naturally assumed it was my idea, which it wasn't.

My trip home to England by car after the England game was to provide me with my one moment of fame. I was travelling down over the A68, the same road I had suffered snow problems with in 1968, and I stopped in Corbridge to go into the bank to withdraw some cash. I needed £5 and in those days there were no bank cards, no cash machines, so I wrote a cheque out at the teller's desk. When she asked me for ID, I began to get out my Army ID card, when the manager behind her said that wasn't necessary because he knew me as he had watched the match on Saturday!

I digress, because the England match, and how I felt before it when the focus was almost entirely on the power of the high ball, really brought back to me the way I had felt for years.

The memory of the mistakes I had made intermittently as a schoolboy and as a student had returned to me with a vengeance. I had suffered mental torture for three days prior to the match after the *Sportsnight* programme.

Onlookers with no similar experience find it impossible to understand what it's like. All they see is an apparently calm player standing waiting to catch a ball that he had known would be coming his way for days.

This, plus the moral pressure of being an absent father for too much of the time, made me decide that season 1970/71, in other words the next season, would be my last in England.

I asked the Army that when it came time to be posted, which was due in November 1971, and whilst that was effectively eighteen months away, could they please send me far away. Germany was no good. I'd already been sent home from there, what I really wanted was a posting to the Far East.

In the meantime there was the small matter of the Scotland tour to Australia in May 1970.

SIXTEEN

You are too fat and idle to play at this level

Selection for the Scotland tour to Australia should have been the prelude to one of the great experiences of my life. I was in good form, flying high, even the English press had been quite subdued, but it turned out to be one of the great disappointments of my life.

It did, however, allow me to meet up again with a man who had been one of the major influences in my rugby career. To do justice to this story I need to return to my university days.

The year is 1967, and I'm desperate to play for Scottish Universities. I'm established in the very good Edinburgh University team, and around twelve of the side are regulars in the Scottish Universities side. My problem is a dental student at Glasgow University called Geoff Allan. He is very strong defensively and definitely first choice, and I know I'd have to go some to take his place. There was also Peter Stott from Aberdeen University who went on to have a very distinguished career with Morgan Stanley amongst others. Peter had great hands and although he wasn't the quickest on his feet, the competition for the full back berth was fierce.

I was very pleased to be asked to attend a Scottish Universities training weekend in St Andrews that was being run by the very distinguished former Scotland and Lions captain, Dr Arthur Smith.

As I wrote previously, I had watched Arthur as a small boy when he was not only in the Scotland team but became a Lion twice in 1955 and 1962, captaining the Lions on the latter tour, having been captain of Scotland since 1960.

The man was a legend, and I was more than a little in awe of him, but it didn't stop me from making a complete fool of myself on the Saturday night. The backs were given time off, whilst the forwards had a blackboard session with Arthur.

I'm afraid a few of us went to the pub and, a little the worse for wear, we barged into the teaching session where I delivered a short homily on the future of back row play. This involved a five foot, one inch number eight who I explained could creep round the back of the scrum, and similarly the lineout, unseen by the referee, causing havoc. At which point Arthur Smith told me my fortune, and that included the words, 'You're too fat and fucking idle to play rugby at this level.'

I thought that was that when I sobered up, but as far as I remember I didn't even apologise.

The next day, the penny dropped. I suddenly realised that it was all very well to be the life and soul of the party but if I wanted to be selected for the Scottish Universities or any other team at a higher level than Edinburgh University I needed to take stock. It was vital to take the game seriously and earn the respect of my elders and betters.

Fortunately, I got one chance to play for the Scottish Universities against Welsh Universities at Craiglockhart in Edinburgh. But I didn't play particularly well and didn't get picked again.

I did, however, manage to get shortlisted for the British Universities side, becoming a non-travelling reserve, but I could never get past Geoff Allan.

Being put firmly in my place by Arthur Smith was one of the hinge moments in my rugby career, and I am forever grateful to him. I was to meet up with Arthur only once more, and that was in Australia in 1970. I had gone there with Scotland as the only full back in the party.

In the first match, against Victoria in Melbourne, towards the end of the second half I caught a high ball. At that moment I received a player with his knees up who caught my wrist and knocked me out because my hands were high to catch the ball and his knee hit my head as well.

X-rays were inconclusive, five doctors split three-two as to whether my wrist was broken or not, and we had to move on to Sydney for our second match, against New South Wales.

The surgeon said I needed a further X-ray in two or three days and that would give a definite diagnosis, but the second X-ray never got taken. Had it been broken there was no question of flying out another full back anyway, because of the time involved and the length of the tour. The fact also was that the SRU were far too mean to go to that kind of expense. You will read evidence of this elsewhere! Having said that, the tour manager Hector Monro had to return home to fight the 1970 General Election, and I don't know who paid for that!

There was little choice but to play on the Saturday against New South Wales, which I did with a heavily strapped wrist. This time I only lasted twenty minutes, when I turned to try to catch John Cole who was at that time one of the top wingers in world rugby. I did manage to tackle him but tore my hamstring in the process.

This injury very much signalled the end of my tour, and the end of the world as far as I was concerned – when out of the blue a gentleman appeared, who told me he was a physiotherapist and that he could get me fit again very quickly using new principles not widely recognised yet in the sports world.

The first thing he did was to sit me on top of a dustbin full of ice and beer, he said to stop the bleed. The injury apparently is smaller than a fingernail, and if you can stop the bleed, and get exercising gently quickly then a cure can be effected. He told me that a very well-known British athlete, Peter Radford, who won a bronze medal in the 200 metres in the Rome Olympics in 1960 had suffered a similar injury ten days before the final, and had followed this guy's treatment recommendation.

I was all ears, and in agony on the ice, where he made me stay for the whole of the second half. He then made me lie on a treatment couch face down while he, in his words, 'broke the contractions' around the injury, which is the body's way of defending itself. Let me tell you, that reduced me to tears such was the pain, as anyone with a hamstring tear knows.

At this point, he told me that if he could have seen me for a week every day I'd be playing in ten days. Unfortunately, he was bound for Mexico on the Monday to be physiotherapist to the England football team during the World Cup.

This was a mighty blow, softened somewhat by an order to attend an address on the Sunday morning on the North Shore in Sydney where he would offer me more treatment. Even before that I needed to start jogging no matter how much it hurt, and boy did it hurt.

Earlier injuries whilst playing for Edinburgh and District, and the Army had found me lacking in help from committee men, but the same thing cannot be said of the Scottish tour management. I was sent in a prepaid taxi to the address, which proved to be an experience by itself. The house contained a concert hall!

In case you think you misread that, you didn't, and this physio, or whatever he was, must have been a multimillionaire. Admittedly this is now some fifty years ago, and the years do play tricks with the memory. One thing I am certain about is the fact that I was ushered into a room, told to strip off, put a towel round myself and to lie on the floor next to a very attractive female athlete also in a state of undress. This man then informed me she was a top sprinter who was going to win medals at the next Olympics in Munich. I think I was lying next to Raelene Boyle, who in fact won two silver medals in the sprints.

The next few minutes are amongst the most agonising I have ever spent as this man proceeded to press his thumbs into the back of my hamstring, followed by the instruction as before to start running immediately. I couldn't even climb on to the team bus without help the next day, never mind jog!

He then abandoned me to go to Mexico, and there I was limping round rugby grounds all over the eastern seaboard of Australia. Eventually the management, understandably fed up with my injury and the others who picked up injuries, sent me to a doctor for a hydrocortisone injection to accelerate the healing process.

For anyone who has ever suffered one of these injections, and I suspect most serious sportsmen and women have at some point, then you will know how quickly the injury appears to heal. I'm not sure if the mental scars heal so quickly because for years after I was convinced my hamstring was going to give way again – but it never did.

I would always apply copious amounts of liniment, often going on to the pitch looking as if I'd been standing in front of a very hot fire. Indeed, I was once described as 'smelling fast'! Fifty years down the road there is still a slight pea-sized lump at the injury site.

To return to the tour, we got to Sydney for the second-last match before the international against Australia, finding ourselves in the situation of not having one replacement. Despite the fact that I could only run at three-quarter speed I was told I had to play, and on no account come off, even if I broke my leg.

Rupert Rosenblum, the Wallaby fly half at that time, was playing and to my great relief he didn't kick one diagonal in the whole match, and I was able to catch, field and kick, without any serious running. When we met in Paris the following January he told me that he had no idea I was injured.

The match against Australia on the Saturday was a disaster, we were well beaten, and one of the worst places to be is in the stand when you know you should have been playing. On my way out at the end of the game I walked into Arthur Smith for the first time since that fateful day when I was a student, and this time there were no insults. He took one look at me and steered me towards a bar, bought two large beers and two large whiskies, and suggested I drank the beer and the whisky down quickly before asking if I felt any better.

I did, a lot better. He told me it had been a good match to miss, selectors always remember the players in a team that loses, and the fact I wasn't playing would help me have a long and successful career. He then added that the other two drinks were for me as well, wished me luck and walked off.

I never saw him again. I discovered later he was in Australia seeking a cure for the cancer he was suffering from. The fact that he took the time at a very difficult moment in his life to comfort me over the small matter of missing a rugby match, says volumes for a wonderful man.

I will never forget him.

SEVENTEEN

We thought Ian very lucky to get his cap last year – but now think he is worth it

By September 1970 I was fit to return to the fray, and it proved to be an amazing start to the year because I found myself at the top of the points-scoring list in England before the end of the month.

Redruth in Cornwall on a London Scottish tour was an exciting start but not for any rugby reason. I had always wanted to play there because of the reputation of 'Hellfire Corner', and the legend of Bonzo Johns, plus more recently the class of Richard Sharp, one of the best fly halves to ever grace the game.

It was what happened before the match, which was a late kick-off on a beautiful Saturday afternoon, that really sticks in the memory. As we sat in the dressing room waiting to go out, the radio was on with the football results being read out. I was doing the football pools at that time, and had a perm of eight from ten, and my first six draws came up. At this point the referee summoned us on to the pitch and, in my high state of excitement, I don't think I missed a kick at goal. Sadly, at full time I discovered my remaining four games had all ended in home wins, so my high expectations came to nothing.

A few weeks later I played for the Army at the Army Apprentice College at Harrogate against a Yorkshire side. This was my first, and not to be last, encounter with Lt Col Mike Hardy, ex-Duke of Wellington's Regiment, and the chairman of the Army selectors. He had played fly half for England alongside Dennis Shuttleworth at scrum half, also a Duke of Wellington's Regiment player.

I failed to see eye-to-eye with Mike, despite kicking the goals that won us the match, and this was to be repeated on more than one occasion. He informed me that the one kick I missed out of seven could have cost the Army the game!

Things were much better at London Scottish as Gordon Macdonald had retired from playing and was in a coaching-cum-management role, and at least we were now talking.

Everything was going well; the English press were even kind to me on a number of occasions and the miss-moves were still working in all the teams I was playing for.

In October, along with a huge number of international players and others, I received a letter asking about my availability for the 1971 Lions tour to New Zealand. As Maureen was pregnant again and due in April, it was an easy decision to make to say no. I was absolutely certain I wasn't good enough to be chosen, but it was nice to be sounded out.

My Army future was looking very much like I would go to Hong Kong in late 1971, so I was happy in my own mind to finish up hopefully playing the whole season for Scotland, and then quietly retire.

Of course, life can never be that simple, and my whole world was to come crashing down in Paris in January 1971.

Prior to that, I had been having a good season at London Scottish, and had scored tries or given scoring passes at key moments against very good sides. We beat Bath 16–14 at Richmond, and I scored a try in the left corner after a miss-move before converting it as the final whistle blew. What I won't forget was Gordon Macdonald kissing me!

We beat London Welsh 16–9 and I was able to give the scoring pass for two tries and kicked all my goals. This was especially good against the very team who many credited with inventing running rugby.

I had been fortunate enough to play in a match in aid of the Pakistan disaster fund. There were seventeen current or past internationalists on the field and a couple of future internationalists, so it was a quality match. I played for the Bosuns, and we beat the Public School Wanderers. I was lucky enough to score a try and kick four conversions, so I knew I was in good form coming up to the trials.

Norman Mair's preview of the first trial in the Scotsman was more than a little interesting if somewhat worrying.

Smith-Blaikie Duel could put selectors in a spot

It took the folk at Richmond a little time to accept Ian Smith; but when I was down there for the Oxford match, I found the general attitude had grown to be as one former international summed up. "We thought Ian very lucky to get his cap last year – but now think he is worth it . . .'

The point, of course, is that last season almost anyone else would have been still luckier, so drastic was the sudden dearth of full backs of the right calibre who were also fit, available, and in their prime.

Though Colin Blaikie was given a torrid time by Finlan when the Herioter last played in an international, the fact remains that when he is in the mood and on song, he can be an embarrassingly gifted and attractive player with whom to stand comparison.

Incidentally one interesting thing about Smith, who did pretty well by Scotland last season, was his unexpected willingness to use, against Oxford, his right foot – which at one time he would almost no sooner have thought of employing to clear than he would his right ear.

That made my thought processes work overtime before the first trial.

Thankfully I won my place in the Scotland team to play France in Paris after facing Colin Blaikie in the trial matches at the end of 1970. This was a very big deal for me, having been in his considerable shadow ever since I left school. I never really felt that I had earned my place the hard way by competing directly against him in front of the selectors. I had now accomplished this, which was a great weight off my mind.

After Robin Marlar's comments about not being international class, and another describing me as one of the five worst international selections ever, I had spent some time dealing with similar comments at work and at training. I had, in truth, forgotten all about it until we played Ireland in 1970. It turned out our Robin had done a character assassination job on Noel Murphy the very famous Irish back row forward a few years earlier. Apparently at the Friday run-out before an Irish match, Noel had gone up to a group of journalists and asked for Robin Marlar. When the individual himself admitted who he was, the story goes that Noel punched him. I don't know how much truth there was in that, but as a story it cheered me up a great deal.

I never achieved that level of satisfaction, and it wouldn't have been my style, but I did get a kind of grudging apology in 1971 a year later after a brief and painful game against France.

My game only lasted 39 minutes.

This was the first time we as players received any 'goodies' in that Adidas supplied us with boots and tracksuits, although we had to pay a nominal sum, something like one-pound sterling to protect our amateur status. How ridiculous is that?

The boots were so comfortable when I trained in them on Friday, so I wanted to wear them for the game itself, but my concern was that I might be called upon as a goal kicker, although with my track record I deemed it unlikely.

I talked to Peter Brown, who was captain and goal kicker, and he said it shouldn't be a problem; he would only not kick if he was exhausted. As this seemed unlikely, I made the decision to play with the boots, and I remember quite clearly how much I enjoyed the atmosphere surrounding the game at Colombes Stadium.

Although the athletic track where Eric Liddell won his Olympic Gold medal separated the crowd from the pitch, the noise when the 'Marseillaise' was sung was unbelievable.

I also remember the bus trip to the ground, done at speed with two police outriders clearing the way with sirens screaming, and a tiny Citroën Dyane tucked in so close behind the bus he got through the crowds through the gates into the stadium as well.

Not for the first time, and possibly not for the last, we were visited by the chairman of selectors in the changing rooms immediately before the match, and on this momentous occasion he was heard to say: 'I've only got five words to say to you boys . . . Claw the c---s down.'

Apart from the language that was only four words, leaving us all more than somewhat confused.

This was the first international match where I felt comfortable with the pace of the game but after about twenty minutes we were awarded a penalty. To my absolute horror Peter called me up to kick for goal. Well it went over, I think off the bar and a post because it was a complete mishit.

Then came disaster. After I kicked a ball to the left-hand touchline about a minute before half-time I was hit late by the French second row Jean-Pierre Bastiat and landed painfully on my shoulder. Substitutes were only made with injury in those far-off days, and the decision rested with the French doctor, who pulled my arm so sharply that our doctor had to stop him, so my game came to an end. We then lost a match I believe we were going to win because, for some inexplicable reason, Brian

Simmers the reserve came on and was put to fly half and Jock Turner, who had been having a magnificent match, was moved to full back.

Back in the seventies there was no question of returning to the dressing room for a hot cup of tea and an earbashing from the coach at half-time. Players stood in a huddle, sometimes to keep warm, and the skipper might say a word. Quartered oranges were brought out, and that was about it. No obsession with hydration and water bottles, and most players would have said, 'No thank you', being frightened of the ignominy of having to leave the pitch for a call of nature. There was no question of a water boy coming on with an earpiece to pass on information from the coach, it was all down to the captain, even though we now had Bill Dickenson from Jordanhill as our equivalent of a coach. Being the SRU, the word coach stank of professionalism, so he was given the grand title of 'Advisor to the Captain'.

I am certain Brian Simmers came on and said he was to go to fly half and Jock to full back, and no one would argue.

After the game I travelled in an ambulance, sirens blaring, to a hospital where I was X-rayed, and the result in beautiful technicolour seemed to show a fracture of my scapula and a shoulder dislocation, which was pretty depressing.

I ended up back at the team hotel long after the boys had gone to the post-match dinner. Having changed, I was on my way out of the door when the hotel receptionist called me and said there was a telephone call for any member of the Scottish team and would I take it. When I picked up the phone this voice said, 'Hello, this is Robin Marlar. I wondered how Ian Smith was?'

'You're speaking to Ian Smith.'

After a moment or two's silence: 'I've been a bit unkind about you in the past.'

'You have, haven't you.'

'Well I thought you were playing very well today until you got hurt, and I hope you'll recover soon.'

This was followed by a complimentary mention in the *Sunday Times* the next day.

Unfortunately, that injury was the beginning of the end of my first-class rugby career, although much of it was self-inflicted.

The technicolour X-ray taken in Paris was repeated on the Monday in the Cambridge Military Hospital in Aldershot, and their opinion was no fracture but a probable dislocation, and although my right shoulder was extremely painful the doctors felt I could play within ten days with appropriate treatment. In fact, I wasn't able to sleep on my right shoulder for over ten years!

The newspaper headline in Scotland on Tuesday, 9 January 1971 read:

Ian Smith may be fit for Wales match

Having had several more x-rays taken on his return to England an elated Ian Smith has been told that the injury inflicted by Bastiat's foul tackle on Saturday is not, after all, a fracture of the scapula.

The verdict now is that his right shoulder bone has been subluxed, which apparently means that there is no actual break, but soft tissue and bruising which cause the pain.

By yesterday morning Smith had regained almost 100 per cent movement, albeit not without such activity still being the reverse of comfortable.

Treatment has already begun and a physiotherapist who has inspected the damage has stated that he would almost be prepared to state his professional reputation that Smith will be fit to play a week on Saturday, on which date London Scottish meet Harlequins. Indeed Smith has not yet withdrawn from an Army match tomorrow week, which makes it distinctly possible he will be available for the game against Wales at Murrayfield on February 6.

The 26 year old Smith a dentist in the Army resumes work tomorrow. Part of his treatment is swimming, starting this morning and already he can do some light training for rugby.

Once almost exclusively left-footed, he throws left armed – but plays tennis and pulls teeth right handed. It is the right shoulder – no longer of course in a sling – that is the casualty.

The Scotland full back has maybe had more than his quota of injuries. That is probably less because he is more injury prone than the next man because – whatever else may be said about him – he has plenty of guts and is always prepared to take what is coming to him. A point his fellow Scotland players are always quick to make and greatly appreciate.

It is at this point in my rugby career that fear and stupidity took over from common sense. I did play within two weeks of the injury, when I knew my shoulder was a long way from being right, and I did make myself available for the game against Wales at Murrayfield.

Looking back, I remember being in fear of losing my place if I didn't play, and then Colin Blaikie was chosen, and starred. Stupidity because I knew my shoulder wasn't right, and I thought I'd get by and not be found out. I should have known better, and in the event I think my injury contributed to Scotland's defeat in a match we could so easily have won, because I failed to make even one tackle, and tackling was always one of my strong points.

In the pre-match team photograph I look like the Hunchback of Notre-Dame such was the size of the shoulder padding I had on.

I then had a game that was so bad, my eldest son thirty years later watching it on video told me he was embarrassed. I dropped a couple of high balls early on, although to be fair they flew kind of funny and then just dropped out of the sky. Barry John told me afterwards he had been experimenting with kicking off the outside of his right foot whilst running left because it imparted spin which made the flight of the ball very different. I then proceeded to not be in quite the right place for most of the Welsh tries so I didn't have to tackle.

The final few seconds saw Gerald Davies go clear on the right wing and, despite a dive, I was never closer than five yards as he scored by the corner flag. We still led 18–17 until the bearded John Taylor, wing-forward extraordinaire, kicked a left-footed conversion to give Wales a 19–18 victory, rightly described as 'the greatest conversion since St Paul on the road to Damascus'.

It was heart-breaking, and worst of all I knew I wasn't fit enough to play at that level and I should have been honest enough to say so, and therefore I was cruelly found out.

Of course, we had the winning of the game when Peter Brown hit the post with a relatively easy conversion of Chris Rea's try, which would have put us 20–14 in front. This would have meant that Wales would have had to score twice.

To be absolutely fair we scored two tries to their four, and Peter had kept us in the game with four superb penalty goals. He told me afterwards that he almost asked me to take the last conversion because he was so tired, and thank goodness he didn't, because I'm not certain the result would even have been as close as the post!

Quite why we threw the ball to Delme Thomas at the final lineout will remain a mystery, and with JPR Williams in the line our defensive plan was that JPR was my man, and Gerald Davies was to be Ali Biggar's responsibility. What actually happened was Ali came hurtling in to try to prevent J.P.R. from getting his pass away, which then left this 'prop' trying to hunt down the best winger in the world.

Alastair did tell me two years later, in the middle of a game in Hong Kong when we were both sitting on the grass watching play go on around us, that he was hopeful at the time for selection for the '71 Lions and he didn't want to be shown up by the electrifyingly quick Davies!

Alastair did of course achieve his goal with the '71 Lions, and rightly so for he was a great player.

I'm lucky because virtually every year when Scotland play Wales that try is shown with the commentator Bill McLaren saying, 'Can Ian Smith get him?' The answer being a very definitive, 'No!'

One more pleasant memory of the morning of the Welsh match was standing with John Frame on Princes Street looking in the R.W. Forsyth's window, where they had a display of rugby memorabilia relating to the Scotland-Wales fixture. Suddenly we realised that the other two figures looking at the window were Gareth Edwards and Barry John. After a smile and a nod, the four of us walked back to the North British Hotel where both teams were based, chatting away, unrecognised by anyone – such was the profile of internationalists in 1971.

When you think about it, unlike today with weekly televised rugby, and the high profile of players on TV, in social media and in the press, the only time the vast majority of people in Scotland would ever see players was on the pitch at internationals or on BBC's *Grandstand*. Therefore, street recognition didn't really happen, at least not in Scotland.

My international career was to ground to an ignominious halt after the Irish match that year, where I threw an intercept pass to seal our defeat. All I remember of that match was in the dressing room after the game when we were sitting around, and the selectors came to have an individual word. As they passed me by they just looked at me and shook their heads in silence. I knew then I was doomed, but even expecting to be dropped doesn't make it any easier when it happens.

EIGHTEEN

You're in the 2nds next Saturday

All good things have to come to an end sometime, and the first bit of writing on the wall can come as a shock. Lt Col Mike Hardy, as chairman of the Army selectors, told me I would be playing on the wing because they wanted to have a look at a youngster called John Davies. This, I may add was after the Welsh and Irish matches.

Hamish Bryce, captain of the Army and Combined Services and a good friend with whom I trained most weeks and played kickabout on any rugby pitch we could find, told me that I was very close to being dropped by both the Army and Combined Services. This was whilst I was still recovering from the damage done to me in Paris against France.

Cheerfully, and Hamish could be very droll, he told me that I was in some danger of doing the treble: being dropped by the Army, Combined Services and Scotland. What he didn't know was I did the quadruple, in that I was to be dropped by London Scottish as well, and all within a ten-day period.

It was the old adage of 'what goes up must come down', but

it was eerie when I look back, that my London Scottish and Scotland career started and ended in almost identical fashion and in the same time frame.

One of the Army selectors was Norman Bruce, who was a most interesting man, very much a rugby fanatic, born in 1932, and sadly now dead. When I first played for the Army in season 1968/69 Norman was thirty-six and officially retired from playing. I remember arriving at Old Deer Park for an Army versus Surrey match and, as Norman got out of his car, I asked him why his rugby kit was in the boot. He told me in no uncertain terms it was just in case someone didn't turn up. As he had been a hooker, that would have been interesting if it had been a winger or a full back who hadn't shown up.

Norman was a very honourable man and during his time as the Scotland hooker he had a long-term reserve, Bob Tollervey, of Heriot's FP.

In those days the reserves travelled but there was no question of substitutes, so unless a player called off at the last moment the reserve had no chance of playing. On one occasion Norman had influenza and rang the Scottish Rugby Union to say he couldn't play. They told him Bob was unavailable because he was ill as well, so Norman said he would play because he wasn't going to allow anyone else to get the cap that Bob deserved. Sadly, Bob never had another chance to win that elusive cap.

As a Scotsman, it was Norman who got the short straw of telling me I had been dropped for the Calcutta Cup match in 1971, and while it didn't come as a surprise it was still a shock. Tact wasn't Norman's best characteristic, but he let me down as gently as he could.

That evening I was sitting at the table eating supper when the phone rang. I said to my wife – more in jest than anything – that it would be Ali Boyle, captain at London Scottish to tell me I'd been dropped by the club. Of course, it was him giving me the news preceded by the word sorry. 'Now you've been dropped by Scotland you're in the 2nds next Saturday.'

The phone call from Ali was just about the last straw and I burst into tears.

I saw Ali a year or so ago at Murrayfield and, even after all these years, it was comforting to hear him say that it was one of the hardest phone calls he'd ever had to make – but he had no option.

Ali was another man I had known since I was a boy. Heriot's played Merchiston Castle from our first year in the senior school, which for them was, I suspect, third form, and their first year at their public school. It was totally boarding, all boys, and the most beautiful grounds surrounding a lovely building up at Colinton in Edinburgh. They beat us consistently, and we used to make the excuse that they practised every day, whereas we only had two practice games a week. Something I have always loved about rugby is the life-long friendships, and Merchistonians like Ali and Sandy Corstorphine are just the loveliest of men.

That was pretty nearly the end of my first-class rugby in England. I sat with a crate of beer in our cottage and watched Scotland beat England at Twickenham, and Arthur Brown at full back hardly touched the ball. He was a hugely talented player, a magnificent seven-a-side exponent, and definitely deserved to be picked. Nevertheless, it wasn't the easiest afternoon watching the match on television, and all these years later I still have difficulty thinking about it.

I turned out for London Scottish 2nds on the following Saturday, on the back pitch, to find myself being barracked, almost sledged to use cricket parlance, by a small group of spectators who jeered every time I touched the ball. They finally left after I kicked two penalties – one from each touchline, about forty yards out from the posts. That was just about it as far as I was concerned with London Scottish, and really stupidly I even made myself unavailable for the team photo for that season.

How senseless pride is, because my two wives have allowed me to have a photo wall consisting of teams I have played for throughout my life, and missing, of course, is anything to do with London Scottish.

NINETEEN

You'll be posted home for not aiding the civilian population

Our posting to Hong Kong was timed for early November 1971, and prior to that I played for Aldershot Services on a couple of occasions when they were short. Their president, Major General Jones, turned out to be the most amazing man. I discovered later he had been described as 'the bravest of the brave' by General Horrocks. As a young captain in 1944, he had defused the mines on the Nijmegen Bridge during the abortive Arnhem attack, almost at point-blank range of the German defenders, for which he was awarded a Military Cross. What a privilege to have known him.

That was the end of my rugby in the UK, and at the time I thought I'd probably never play again, which didn't bother me. Little did I know I would continue to play on and off for another ten years.

We left RAF Brize Norton in early November in total innocence of what we were heading into. It is hard to believe in the twenty-first century that we were not to be able to speak on the telephone to our parents when we were in Hong Kong. Today everyone has a mobile phone and you can speak, and even see the person you're speaking to, anywhere in the world at any time, and depending on your contract, the call is free. In 1971 there were only landlines and the calls were prohibitively expensive for a young Army dentist and his wife. As a result, we didn't speak to our parents for well over a year, until they came to visit.

Today a flight to Hong Kong takes slightly less than thirteen hours non-stop. In 1971, flying in a Royal Air Force VC10, the journey took I think about twenty-four hours with a couple of stops on the way, including RAF Gan in the Maldives, and Singapore. It was a very long way with a seven-month-old baby and a twenty-one-month-old little boy.

We arrived in Hong Kong minus rugby boots, which was deliberate. What was accidental was the fact that I managed to leave behind the most critical suitcase with the children's nappies! In 1971, disposable nappies were but a pipe dream as far as we were concerned, so we couldn't just go out and buy some more. All nappies were towelling with liners and they were expensive. They required washing every day, and to put them on required no little skill with a huge safety pin so as not to stab the poor baby. To leave such an important case behind was not the best start to our new life.

Within a few days I received a phone call asking me to be a guest at a club rugby match. I told the caller I probably wouldn't be playing any rugby, but I was reassured the invitation was only to watch. There were several home-based threats about what would happen if I even thought about playing again.

It doesn't take much guesswork to know what happened next, of course. A few beers down I agreed to play the following Saturday. I was, as ever, very concerned, because they wanted me to play at full back, and the game I had watched under the lights at the Hong Kong Football Club had been played at a ferocious pace. I also noticed how there was little or no grass on the pitch, and despite it being November how warm it was compared to the UK and how the playing surface was very dry.

I hadn't trained and, quite honestly, I thought I'd probably make a total fool of myself. As you can imagine, Maureen was somewhat angry, as I had convinced her my rugby days were over, but of course at only twenty-seven years of age that was never going to happen.

My nerves before the game were as bad as anything I'd ever experienced, then the first two times I got the ball and started running I scored tries. I'm still not convinced it wasn't a set-up to convince me that I could still play!

The only conclusion I could draw was that the standard just wasn't very good, and of course I was only eight months away from playing first-class rugby in England, so I probably shouldn't have been surprised.

Fairly quickly I was asked to captain Army Hong Kong, which I was more than happy to get involved in, but it became obvious that there was a selection committee who were picking players I felt weren't good enough.

After a discussion which was full and frank, the committee disbanded, and I could pick the players I wanted. At one stage in the negotiations it was agreed that the committee would pick the team, I would then have the last word on selection, but this proved unworkable.

The biggest problem was the fact that the chairman, Lt Col Arthur Edwards (a former Welsh international full back) and I did not get on. As a ten-year old, I remember watching him when Scotland broke their run of seventeen consecutive defeats in 1955. This was when Arthur Smith made a bit of a fool of him to score a wonderful individualistic try which turned the match. I'm afraid I was too opinionated, and it was a mistake to turn away all of Arthur's advice and experience, but I suppose it was the impetuosity of youth. He was to get a measure of revenge later.

Captain John Grigsby was the secretary of Army Hong Kong Rugby, and he was in the Royal Signals. A real old-fashioned professional soldier he took no sides in my sometimes-heated discussions with Arthur Edwards. What he did do was to install a telephone in my office that was purely for rugby calls, and all the army players in Hong Kong knew the number. This made such a difference when it came to organising training and match selections and sometimes, in fact, not infrequent call-offs.

Hong Kong isn't large but when I arrived it was quite difficult to get around. It consisted of Hong Kong Island, Kowloon Peninsula, and then the New Territories.

The New Territories were on a ninety-nine-year lease, and started at Boundary Street in Kowloon. The lease expired in 1997, which was still a long way off in 1971.

The British Garrison was spread from Stanley Fort on the south side of the island, where I was to be working, right up to the border with China. The problem, insofar as rugby was concerned, was that the Army rugby pitch was at King's Park in Kowloon next to the British Military Hospital. To get there from Hong Kong Island in season 1971/72 was a long journey which required getting on a harbour car ferry as, at that time, there was no tunnel connecting the island to Kowloon until August 1972. For my rugby players based on the island who wanted to drive, it could be a ninety-minute journey to the ground, and sometimes even longer at weekends because of traffic volume and queues for the ferry.

As an aside, it could take a lot longer if, like me, you drove a very old Ford Corsair, with no silencer and a lousy battery. On one occasion I left the headlights on in the car whilst crossing the harbour on the Yaumati ferry. As my car was due to be first to drive off, with a flat battery and the ramp being uphill, I leave you to imagine the chaos that followed!

Thanks to the need to use the ferry at this time it meant frequent call-offs from players based on the island and if we were playing at the football club on the island it was even tougher for players based in the New Territories.

It is important to realise the rugby that was played, while taken seriously, wasn't anything like the priority in players' lives it was at home in the UK. The Army also had the annoying habit of insisting that duty came before rugby. The military doesn't just work Monday to Friday either, so my telephone dramatically reduced the chances that Army teams would turn up short. In addition, I was incredibly fortunate to work in the middle of an infantry battalion, so replacements could always be found, even if not always to the standard I wanted – but occasionally real gems were unearthed.

At the start of the 1972/73 season there was great excitement about the forthcoming Asian Rugby Games in November 1972, and Hong Kong were fancying themselves to do well. The Colony team had a good coach in Dennis Evans, one of the unluckiest players ever to wear a Welsh jersey.

He was capped only once – on the wing against Avril Malan's Springboks in 1960 – at a time when the winger threw in at the lineout, and that was the only time that Dennis touched the ball. There had been torrential rain, the Taff had overflowed its banks and Cardiff Arms Park was virtually under water. A gale-force wind was blowing up and down the pitch, and Wales held the Springboks to a single penalty in the first half with the big wind advantage in the second half. Sadly for Wales they simply didn't win enough ball in the second half and never put the Springboks under any pressure at all. The Springboks duly won 3–0 and poor Dennis never did a thing wrong yet he was never picked again.

His plan was to take the Colony squad away at weekends for training sessions in Sek Kong in the New Territories, but I had promised Maureen I had finished with all that sort of thing, so I said I wouldn't go.

At this the proverbial shit hit the fan. Maureen was pressured to make me go, and it all culminated in a phone call in a restaurant one lunchtime from Arthur Edwards. Quite how he knew where we were I will never know. He said to Maureen, 'You'll be posted home for not aiding the civilian population.'

As you might imagine, my wife told me to get it sorted in no uncertain terms. Basically it was down to choices, so there was no choice! Life in Hong Kong was very comfortable for officers' wives because we had full time live-in Chinese amahs to cook and to look after the children, which, after the pressures of small babies in the UK, was like paradise on earth.

The gist of the call was that if I continued to refuse to go to Sek Kong at weekends for Colony training sessions, and thus make myself unavailable for the Asian Games, I would be reported to the Commander British Forces, who would have me sent back to England in disgrace. If this happened, it would be my military future on the scrapheap. Apparently one of the key things for the troops in Hong Kong was aiding the civilian population.

Lt General Sir Richard Ward did not bear fools gladly I was told. After Arthur hung up it made me more determined than ever to stand up for myself. After all, I had been posted to Hong Kong as a dental officer not a rugby player.

Arthur Edwards was Chief Education Officer and journeyed to work every day in the same staff car as my Colonel, one Frank Ashenhurst, who was Chief Dental Officer. An Irishman and not unsympathetic to my feelings, Frank told me to get a compromise worked out asap, because Lt Colonels are answerable to Lt Generals and he had a career path too!

At this point a lovely South African called Tokkie Smith intervened. His main claim to fame is the fact that he was the man who founded the Hong Kong Sevens. In 1972 he was playing a role in the organisation of Hong Kong Rugby, only

I didn't realise that. Tokkie came to my rescue when he called and told me he knew of my predicament and thought he had a solution.

Tokkie felt it was all very well for the Colony team to go to Sek Kong in the New Territories training, but a game would be much better practice for them. In fact, Dennis Evans had welcomed his suggestion to field a rest of Hong Kong XV against what would be the starting XV for Hong Kong in the Asian Games.

Tokkie then asked if I would agree to play in that match even if I did nothing else. He also felt that just doing that would take some of the pressure off me regarding the Army.

Rugby in Hong Kong in the early 1970s was confined to three big teams, the Hong Kong Football Club, the Police and the Army, with the Royal Navy and RAF Kai Tak making up the five teams who played in the Pentangular competition. Club and Police may have fielded second teams. In addition, there were service teams as well including 48 Brigade in the New Territories and 51 Brigade on the island, plus unit sides like the Irish Guards and the Black Watch.

Taking the best players for the Colony team left very few decent players to pick to play against them. I remember all too well pleading with club 2nd XV players, who were expatriates working in Hong Kong who just played a bit of rugby for fun, to turn out.

Anyway, the game took place and to everyone's surprise the Rest of Hong Kong beat the Hong Kong side 15–12. It was one of the most fun and best games I have ever been involved in, and players who should have been out of their depth responded to the challenge incredibly well. I can't remember the scorers, but I may have been lucky enough to score all our points.

As you can imagine, after the match I was pretty happy when I sat on the steps outside the changing rooms removing my boots. Dennis Evans, after complimenting our team, told me that all bets were off, and that he'd be very happy if I just played, and there was no need to give up my weekends.

I just remember how pleased I was to have been allowed to stay on in Hong Kong. It had been a very uncomfortable few weeks because I really wanted to play in the Asian Rugby Games, I just didn't want all the squad training that went with it.

It was a wonderful experience to take part in the Asian Games, and we beat Thailand and South Korea to qualify to play Japan in the final. Hong Kong had a good side, being able to field three ex-internationals in Alastair Biggar, Paul Gibbs (Australia) and me, whilst our pack had a sprinkling of players with first-class experience.

It has to be said that Japan were simply too good. They had recently been on a successful tour of New Zealand and I believe their two wings, Tadayuki Ito and Demi Sakata, had been nominated as players of the year there. One thing was certain, while the Japanese were small in stature they were so quick and inventive, much of the time we were left chasing shadows.

There were two things in particular I remember about the Japan team. The first was their lineout technique, because they had to counter the size of Paul Selway-Swift in our second row, and the way they accomplished this was fascinating. A command was given in Japanese, and at this point their thrower turned his back on the touchline and started to walk away. The code was obviously the number of paces he took before turning and firing the ball at rocket-like speed low to their front jumper who was in the air as the ball arrived. He didn't catch it, just deflected it to the scrum half, and the ball was in the fly half's hands before we had even blinked. It was amazing and delivered with well-honed pinpoint accuracy.

The second thing was the way the ball was delivered to their wingers. Our wing would be marking his man, but the Japanese winger would start running in a wide arc before the flat hard pass was delivered, not forward but so close to being forward that when the wing received it he was already outside his man. It was the closest thing I have ever seen to the through ball in soccer, and boy was it effective. I see it now in some of the big spin passes fired out wide in internationals today by exponents like Finn Russell, Owen Farrell, Danny Cipriani and George Ford, but at that time I had never seen anything like it.

We lost 16–0 and the local press in the *South China Morning Post* had a field day attacking the team, the selection policy and the training routine. Some things don't change with the press. They do love to minutely dissect the failings of a losing national team! As far as I remember, the team were pretty angry about that, and I remember writing a letter which was published, complaining about the ignorance of the press. After all, we were a bunch of guys in Hong Kong, who were there to work and further our professional careers and for whom rugby was a hobby to be played and enjoyed on a Saturday. Whilst many of us had experienced success previously we were no longer as fit, as quick or as dedicated as we once were.

Looking back at the Japanese, I do think it was one of my first experiences of the way rugby was beginning to develop, with the sheer professionalism of the Japan team.

The Asian Games ended in a very moving ceremony with a lone piper standing on top of one of the grandstands illuminated by a spotlight playing 'Amazing Grace'.

TWENTY

The Irish Guards don't play rugby

My posting in Hong Kong was to the 1st Battalion, Irish Guards, who were based on the south side of Hong Kong Island at a most lovely place called Stanley Fort. I had possibly one of the most beautiful environments as a workplace in the world. I was also in sole charge of a dental centre overlooking the sports field.

Looking straight ahead, in the distance was the blue South China Sea with an island on the horizon which apparently contained a Chinese army gunnery range zeroed in on Stanley Fort! To my right, and reasonably close by, was again blue sea and getting to work in the morning was a ten-minute drive along the coast with a number of startlingly beautiful views. I was really in paradise for two and a half years, and better still was the fact that there were to be three rugby seasons. Initially this was never discussed with Maureen!

Rugby in Hong Kong generally was one of the most enjoyable experiences of my life. Initially I was frustrated by the fact that the two pitches I could see outside my surgery were football pitches, and initial enquiries when I joined the Irish Guards were met with the words, 'The Irish Guards don't play rugby.'

The football pitch outside my surgery quickly became a rugby pitch, and the Irish Guards, whose teeth I was responsible for, began to play rugby largely because of an officer called Brian O'Farrell who had played for Dublin Wanderers.

Once again, I was in a service rugby environment, representing 51 Brigade, which was one of the two Brigades stationed in Hong Kong, the other being 48 Brigade, based at Sek Kong, and also Army Hong Kong and the Irish Guards. This was my third experience of rugby in the Army after BAOR and then unit rugby in the UK and full Army representation. Once again it was very different to anything I had experienced before.

Wherever there is the British Army there must be an Army Cup, and Hong Kong was no exception. I remember the Irish Guards struggling to beat 1st Battalion, Black Watch, in the semi-final, a game we only won because of a sergeant called Jimmy Mooney who was an Army footballer. Awarded a penalty forty yards out to the right-hand side of the posts, I asked Jimmy if he thought he could kick it. His reply indicated it wasn't a problem and was vindicated with a beautifully struck left-foot kick. A few minutes later from the same range on the other side of the posts, he repeated the same success, only this time with a right-foot kick, and because of that we won, 12–9.

Modern players have no idea how difficult it was to take a place-kick forty or fifty years ago. You had to tee the ball up by making indentations in the turf with the heel of your boot, to all four points of the compass, and then with your hands try to seat the ball on the mound of earth you had created.

I can tell you that in Hong Kong the pitches tended to be rock hard which made it a whole lot tougher, but all Jimmy did was to make a small hole, sit the ball upright, take a few paces back and *bang*!

We were due to play 48 Brigade, Minor Units, in the final at the Army pitch at King's Park in front of the military hospital.

The fact was that in a recent friendly warm-up fixture the 48 Brigade, Minor Units, had demolished the Black Watch, scoring over fifty points in the process.

Their team consisted of fourteen officers and one private soldier; the 'Micks' side was made up of twelve guardsmen and three officers, so the omens were not good. Looked at objectively, the fourteen officers, probably mostly from a public school background, would have been brought up playing rugby, whereas the majority of our guardsmen were converts from the round ball game.

We looked to be on a hiding to nothing, but I had no experience in my life before, and certainly never since, of what was about to happen.

Before the match in the dressing room I listened in awe to Brian O'Farrell's team talk; although strictly speaking as the captain it was my function, there was no way I could ever do what he did.

Brian's team talk was a real call to arms as Irish Guardsmen, and it made me realise the close-knit bond all ranks in an infantry battalion have. It made me stop and think that had things gone wrong between us and the Chinese that Brian and others like him would have to lead these men into what would have been a war zone with huge casualties, and I felt really humbled to be present.

Looking at the 48 Brigade side as they arrived, and I knew most of them quite well, they seemed almost arrogant. It was almost as if they thought that all they had to do was turn up – but the Micks were spoiling for a fight thanks to Brian.

Memory plays tricks but I think at one point we led something like 15–0, and we were coasting. Then the Micks began to show off, as only a bunch of Irishmen could, and we very nearly let our opponents back into the game. After a few well-chosen words from Brian, they knuckled down and we ran out easy winners.

In all my rugby career this was one of the real genuine highlights. Between Brian O'Farrell, Roger Belson, Julian Mellor, and a group of guardsmen with little rugby experience, we had beaten the best that the Army in Hong Kong had to offer. I can tell you we partied hard afterwards in downtown Kowloon!

In addition, we had got a rugby pitch re-established at Stanley Fort, which remained until the British handed over the barracks to the Chinese. This was despite the fact that the Irish Guards at that time were not known as a rugby playing regiment, but far more for football and boxing. In fact, there is still a rugby club in Hong Kong called Valley Fort, and I feel I had a part, albeit a very small part, in helping that club to have a pitch to play on.

When 1 Kings, who are basically a Liverpool regiment, arrived to replace the Irish Guards, they were very keen to play rugby, and with Jeremy Gaskell, a former Army player as adjutant and Major Colin Denning captaining the side, there was every chance we could win the Army Cup again.

However, the consequences of games like this between brothers in arms can be like a family feud where friends and relatives fall out, and even come to blows. We had to play an Ordnance side in the semi-final, captained by Noel Barker, who was an Army and Colony teammate as well as a friend. We had got to the ground first and then Noel's team arrived, and as per usual I said hello to him, to be completely ignored, and the same thing applied to the rest of his team, several of whom I knew and played with anyway. This came as a total surprise, and certainly their belligerence in the opening few minutes bordered on violence.

We were somewhat lucky to win, and I had the good fortune to drop three goals from a long way out, not I may add in open play but as penalties, the ground being too hard to get a decent hole to sit the ball in. This certainly didn't please my friend Noel one little bit, and even after the final whistle he was still muttering about injustice, flukes and all sorts. He did smile again but it took him several weeks.

I can't for the life of me remember who we played in the final, but I know this much, which was that I was running a temperature, and it was a warm day, so I really suffered, but winning made it worthwhile.

It was fantastic to play in another regimental team, again better known for soccer, and to win another land forces cup.

Prior to the arrival of 1 Kings, I was approached to write rugby reports by the *Hong Kong Standard* who were then the number two English language newspaper. I was also told that if that went well, then there might be an opportunity to write for the number one paper, the *South China Morning Post* (*SCMP*).

There was one small problem and that was the word 'professionalism'. At that time, if you were paid for doing anything in connection with rugby you were branded a professional. This meant that from that moment on you were banned from ever playing rugby union again, and you were even banned from ever entering a rugby clubhouse. This was all seriously draconian, but nevertheless the rebel in me saw this as a challenge.

It was obvious I had to write incognito, and I would do so under the name of Peter Stewart. Arrangements were made to pay the small amount I would earn into a branch of HSBC in Stanley Village, but there was one seemingly insurmountable obstacle and that was I would have to learn to type.

It became fun sneaking away from the after-match beers going to the newspaper office, and in the beginning I tried to print my match account by hand. Unfortunately, whoever was responsible for typing that out was, I suspect, Chinese and without much English, so what appeared made no sense at all.

Typing had to be done on an old-fashioned typewriter, whose keyboard was almost vertical, the kind of things you find in antique auctions nowadays. Every error had to be laboriously corrected, and it took two hours to do every Saturday evening.

I have to say I loved writing the reports and listening to my teammates and opponents discussing them in the bar the following week. I think I enjoyed the secrecy as much as anything, and it was nice to express an opinion without having to justify it. The question, of course, did arise as to the identity of the author. The fact that I was frequently and heavily criticised in the newspaper deflected any guesses as to who it was away from the chance it might be me.

The problem eventually arose, however, when some bright individual realised that the only matches reported on were ones that I was involved in, so I had to find a confidante I could trust and ask him to watch a Police versus Club match and give me a report! I eventually decided that Peter Stewart had to be killed off and replaced by Gordon Steven.

This worked after a fashion, and I thought I had got away with it, and with my time in Hong Kong drawing to a close I had heard two whispers, the first was the *Morning Post* wanted me to write for them, and second that I was to captain the Hong Kong Colony XV.

One evening our doorbell rang, which was very uncommon. We lived on the eighth floor of a block of flats called Garden Mansions which overlooked Repulse Bay, and the views were spectacular.

On opening the door, I found Jack Johnson, a senior police officer, an official in the Hong Kong Rugby Football Union, and one of the better referees in the colony. My first hopeful thought that he might be here to ask me to be Colony captain was shattered when he refused a drink, saying he was on official business.

What he went on to say was that they, and I assume by 'they' he meant the Hong Kong RFU committee, knew I was Peter

Stewart and Gordon Steven. They also knew I had been offered the *SCMP* job and as far as captaincy was concerned they were not going to have me controlling Hong Kong Rugby. I was left with one choice, and that was to stop writing for the *Standard*, and refuse the *SCMP* or I would never be Colony captain as I would be branded a professional.

That was that, although one touch of light relief was that a whole year after returning to England I discovered the *Standard* had gone on paying me, which just goes to show how little they noticed my efforts in the first place!

Club rugby in Hong Kong was dominated by the Hong Kong Football Club, and the main competition was the Pentangular which included the Police and the Army as the main opposition, and although the Navy and the RAF also played they were minor opponents.

The Army against Police, and Army versus Club matches could be stormy affairs, and there were two epic battles that fondly remain in my memory.

Most of the Police side were resident in Kowloon and our home pitch King's Park was in Kowloon. This made it almost like a home fixture for the Police, so I decided we should play them at Stanley Fort to make it as difficult as possible. The reason for this was simple: it meant they had to work their way through the Harbour Tunnel and then fight through the traffic from Central District down to Repulse Bay and then into Stanley Fort, which is on the south side of the island. When they arrived at the guardroom they needed an ID card check. All extremely inconvenient and time consuming, so they weren't happy bunnies when told this was what they had to do.

When kick-off time arrived they had no shirts, and asked for a delay for thirty minutes, and being a kind person, I said, 'You'll have to play without your jerseys,' and the game had to start promptly or I would claim the points.

The Police played for most of the first half in skins, and on a pitch that wasn't exactly free of small stone chips. I was definitely hunted down by Mike Francis, a very good open side wing forward, who accidently (of course) hit me late on several occasions. Gus Cunningham, one of the most sporting players I ever played with or against anywhere, did at least see the funny side of it, but that was some time later. My memory of a notable victory remains.

We forced the Football Club to travel up to Sek Kong, which was a long way for the city slickers, most of whom lived on Hong Kong Island, and they were definitely not pleased at all. The game proved to be possibly the most violent I played in during my three seasons in Hong Kong, but if my memory serves me well we won this as well.

Another rugby highlight was the only time I have ever been on a rugby pitch and tried to lose. It came to light in 1974 that there were enough Heriot's former pupils in Hong Kong to raise a seven-a-side team to play in a competition known as the Blarney Stone sevens, which took place at the Football Club.

I can't remember who we played in the first round but what I do know is that it went to a third period of extra time. Don't be misled, it wasn't due to our efforts to win. Neither side wanted to win because both teams were strictly in it for fun, and we knew our second-round opponents were to be the Hong Kong Football Club's 1st seven, who were the overwhelming favourites. There was one farcical moment when one of our forwards broke clear on the halfway line, realised to his horror that no one was chasing him, and the line was clear in front of him, so he tried to drop a goal – and missed.

It wasn't just on the rugby field that life in Hong Kong was interesting, there were some other things that happened that were quite unbelievable. When I first arrived with Maureen, eighteen-month-old Simon, and seven-month-old Mark, we didn't have enough 'points' to qualify for an official army flat, known as a quarter. This meant we had to look on the local Chinese market and rent a flat which we paid a small fortune for. It was in Chung Hom Kok Road very close to Stanley village and Stanley Fort.

We were innocents abroad, and the flat we rented had no furniture, no carpets, holes in the wall for air conditioning which we couldn't afford, so we had to hire everything from chairs and tables to a cooker and fans.

In our ignorance we didn't know how hot it got in the summer and we made sure we had a west-facing balcony to enjoy the evening sun. However, it got so hot that the thermometer we had on the balcony exploded during our first summer there! There was no question of sitting out.

During our time in Chung Hom Kok, the block of flat's caretaker murdered the amah of a neighbour, David Ford, who was working in PR for the Army and the Hong Kong government. He is now Sir David Ford, having left the Army to become the last expatriate chief secretary of Hong Kong. He and his wife went away for a weekend and when they returned they found their amah murdered with all the knives in the house in her throat. Our caretaker was found guilty on the evidence of fingerprints on a coke bottle. It was quite chilling because the caretaker used to chat up our amah, and often carried Mark, who was then a small baby, around in his arms.

Also during that time in 1972, we had rain quite unlike anything I had ever experienced before. We were living in the same flat which had a roof area where we had installed a paddling pool. The rain was so heavy the paddling pool filled up every hour and the rain carried on in the same way for around forty-eight hours. Someone told me that forty-eight inches of rain fell in seventy-two hours, and as a consequence a major block of flats in Mid-levels collapsed and a large number of people were killed, not only there but all over Hong Kong. We certainly couldn't get out of our road which was blocked by a landslide.

Partly as a result of this we were allocated a service flat, a quarter, and we were sure it was to be in either Garden Mansions or Roydon Court, both lovely blocks of flats overlooking Repulse Bay. Well, we found out we were not going to be there, but much further towards town, and when we went to look, the flats were tiny, with no balconies and no air conditioning. In fairness we had never been able to afford air conditioning, but fans and open balcony sliding windows in the summer made life tolerable if you overlooked the sea, which we did in Chung Hom Kok.

This flat we were to be put into looked at a cliff face; no chance of a breeze here, and the bathroom was so small that only one person could use it at a time.

I was furious, but help came from an unexpected quarter. There was an annual fixture when the CBF's XV (Commander British Forces) played the Taipans XV and the teams were all introduced to the Deputy Director Land Forces, Major General 'Bunny' Burnett by Lt Col Arthur Edwards. When my turn came to shake hands with the General he asked me how I was enjoying Hong Kong, and I told him I loved it, 'But we'd just been allocated a quarter that wasn't up to scratch.'

Now it is very much a service tradition not to complain to Generals and certainly not at a sporting event, so I had really spoken out of turn. The General seemed completely unperturbed, and asked me why, so I told him. Arthur Edwards looked daggers at me, and on the Monday I received a summons to my Colonel's office. As mentioned earlier, my Colonel was Lt Col Frank Ashenhurst, a typical Ulsterman who deservedly ended up as the Major General Director Army Dental Service. Sadly, he died a few years ago and I regarded him as a good friend.

We did have a history before I was ever posted to Hong Kong from one night at a regimental dinner in the officers mess in Aldershot when he was a major, which definitely ranks above a junior captain which I was. It was my duty to call him sir, but on this occasion in a somewhat drunken state I called him 'Frankie Baby', and his response was along the lines of, 'If you ever get posted under my command I'll fix you, so just hope it never happens!'

It did, and I was very flattered to be told in Hong Kong by another dental officer that he had said how much he was looking forward to my arrival because I was just the kind of officer he wanted to complete his team!

Before returning to my sorry tale about the general I should also add that Colonel Frank used to hold dental officer training days on a Saturday when he encouraged misbehaviour, and on one occasion he bet me I couldn't go down a particular street in Kowloon without touching the pavement. This meant climbing over the tightly packed cars, which I managed, but it had unfortunate consequences later on in my life.

He had a lovely wife called Hilary, and at the end of these drunken dental escapades on a Saturday, somehow he always suggested I ensure he got home safely. This meant entering his flat and, to quote Rabbie Burns, 'Where sits his sulky sullen dame, gathering her brows like gathering storm, nursing her wrath to keep it warm.'

Now Hilary was one of the nicest people you could ever wish to meet, another lovely Ulster girl. However, I realised fairly quickly that the reason Frank asked me to go home with him was so he could blame me for the lateness of the hour and his less than sober condition! Hilary's ultimate revenge apparently was to make herself raw garlic sandwiches and eat them immediately Frank appeared!

Anyway, he had the fortune (or misfortune) of sharing a staff car every morning to work with Arthur Edwards, who gave him chapter and verse about the appalling behaviour of one of his junior officers. Talk about revenge being a dish best served cold!

I was duly summonsed to an interview, as they say, without coffee, and my behaviour not only on this one occasion, but on several other occasions, was gone over in fine detail. Less than a week later the flat we had been allocated was downgraded to a sergeant's quarter and we were allocated B8 Garden Mansions in Repulse Bay. This block of flats overlooked the South China Sea with enormous accommodation including three big bedrooms, an en-suite with a balcony you could hold a party on, and views to die for.

Three months later, Major General Burnett was on an official inspection of Stanley Fort and during this he had of course to inspect the Dental Centre. When the Irish Guards commanding officer said to him that he wouldn't know the Dental Officer, Captain Ian Smith, the general just smiled and said we were old friends, and how did I like my accommodation!

The very last rugby I played in Hong Kong was a tour to Japan and Korea in 1974. I only played in the two Japan matches because it was so close to my posting back to the UK that I couldn't finish the tour. It was a memorable trip, seeing the blossom at the ancient palace of Kyoto, and having a sauna followed by a body wash and massage in our hotel. We did play rugby too, but first the tale of the sauna.

Our hotel had this deal going where you had a fifteen-minute sauna, followed by the body wash and massage for a very small amount of money. Me and two teammates, who will remain anonymous, took up the offer. They came, as I remember, because I had a Diners Club card which got a special rate!

I'd never had a sauna before, and barely lasted the fifteen minutes, in fact if they hadn't locked us in I'd have fled before the time was up; it was hotter than anything I had ever experienced before. We were told to take a cold plunge before the body wash, and as we came out of the sauna the cold bath on the left was packed so I jumped into the pool on the right which turned out to be the hot tub, and as I was naked you don't have to guess what got the most burnt.

The rugby was intense as always against the Japanese international players. It was a novel experience to play in Japan, and at fly half for the first time in an international against a country who were beginning to get full internationals against IRB countries.

It's like many important things in your life that happen, and you don't appreciate the significance of it for years and years. It was only recently when I had a communication from the Hong Kong RFU asking me when I would be able to be in Hong Kong to receive my international cap, because since 1997 Hong Kong has been regarded by World Rugby as a country that can award caps. Suddenly you think to yourself, 'That's pretty special to be the proud owner of caps for two countries.'

It was around that time that the using of a wall at a short penalty came into vogue. I believe it was started in Australia, where the whole team stood in a line as a wall with their backs to the opposition, some yards behind where the penalty was to be taken, with the scrum half on the ball. He would tap it to himself, pass to the end person in the wall and run behind the wall, whereupon the wall turned round, all with their hands stuck up inside their jerseys to look like the ball, and scattered running towards the opposition try line. The confusion meant no one knew who had the ball and a try was almost a formality.

This was outlawed pretty quickly by the IRB to maintain their reputation as lacking in humour, but it didn't stop sides from amending it to make it legal. The most common technique was for the scrum half to be on the ball, which was placed five or ten yards behind the spot indicated by the referee. As the opposition had to be some ten yards from the penalty it ensured no one could reach the ball carrier before the ball went behind the wall and then reappeared, because that would have meant a penalty for obstruction.

The penalty would really only be taken when there was a substantial blind side so the three-quarters could be split, although as part of the double bluff it was common to load the three-quarters on one side. The scrum half would pass to the end man in the wall, who would either give it back to him as he ran round behind the wall to link with the backs, or not, if they were on the other side.

The fly half would very often stand behind the wall, hidden from view and either take the ball back towards the penalty spot and link with the forwards, or the forwards would keep the ball and perhaps move it to the third person in the wall, who would then turn and charge.

Well, against Japan we tried a variation where I got the ball, hopefully in the clear as we had tried one or two variations with limited success. On this occasion I came round the wall to be faced by three grinning Japanese players who dumped me unceremoniously on my backside. I don't think we tried it again!

We lost to Japan (again), and then for my last game in a Hong Kong jersey I was given the captaincy against a select XV. I can remember being very emotional, and in fact was in tears at the end. I had so enjoyed my rugby in the Far East. I had escaped from full back once and for all, no more the 'slower than your average prop' full back as I was much slower than your average prop by then and coming into the line from full back would no longer have been an option.

I loved playing but was beginning to get more enjoyment in helping other players to play to their potential, and planning matches.

At one stage I was asked if I could help train some boys from St Stephen's College at Stanley next to the Army camp I worked at. St Stephen's College was, at that time, a private school with students from all over the Far East. The biggest problem was that I couldn't bring them into Stanley Fort where we had the rugby pitch next to the Dental Centre, so I had to teach them on an area of grass not much bigger than a volleyball court.

As you can well imagine, while this wasn't an impossible task it was made harder by the inconsistency of attendance, and also the fact that I had to draw the pitch out on the sandy ground to try to explain what would happen when we played a match.

The team captain was a stocky lad from Thailand, and he was almost the only boy who spoke and understood English. We had one or two matches, but invariably kids would turn up I had never seen before, and that made the whole exercise pretty hopeless.

One Saturday we got the fantastic opportunity to play against the second team from King George V School from Kowloon, a very British school. Of course, the usual thing happened and a lad turned up to play I hadn't seen before. The captain assured me this lad was good and, as we only had a team of fifteen players, he had to play despite my concerns. The game was to be played on the pitch at Stanley Fort and we got special permission from the commanding officer to allow the civilian children and their parents into the military base.

Well what an eye-opener, this boy was a total natural. He was playing at outside centre and the first time he got the ball he ran past his opposite number as if he wasn't there. He then ran over the try line close to the corner flag; the only problem then was he kept running over the dead-ball line and up the hill behind.

The very understanding referee brought him back and awarded the try while we tried to explain about the try line and the dead-ball line. Anyway, he asked to take the kick, after we had explained what to do, and he kicked a beautiful conversion from the touchline with his left foot.

Later in the game he repeated his try-scoring feat, this time on the other side of the posts, and once again, but from the opposite touchline and with his right foot, he kicked another inch-perfect conversion. What a talent, but sadly I never saw him again.

One of the delights of rugby in Hong Kong was the fact I managed to get the Army team kit washed at Stanley Fort along with the regimental sports kit at the Dhobi Wallah, which was really the soldier's laundry at the back of the camp facing the sea. I was finally caught out as it was all supposed to be paid for by me; what the authorities didn't know was that the Irish Guards, and then 1 King's had been paying for it for almost three seasons. What was even better was they didn't ask for any money retrospectively!

Leaving Hong Kong in May 1974 was a very sad time; I had really loved it. I wasn't at all sure if that was the right thing for me. I desperately wanted a successful army career, and I had run my own dental centre for the past thirty months. I was going home to Pirbright in Surrey to run a slightly bigger dental centre, and that was exciting enough; I couldn't see much beyond that.

Success in the Army only meant one thing to me and that was becoming the top man, and that was a major general. To get there you really needed to get on with people who mattered, and that already wasn't my strong suit.

In late 1972 the then president of the HKRFU, Vernon Roberts, asked me if I would be interested in leaving the Army and remaining in Hong Kong. The idea was very appealing until I looked at the costs involved in private renting. We were very spoiled in the Army with superb flats and I knew we couldn't afford anything as grand. Also with two small children and education to think about I regretfully declined his offer of floor space in one of his downtown offices to open a dental practice.

I've often wondered what would have happened had I stayed, but on the principle of never looking back, there are so many things in my life I would have missed had I stayed.

One of the final acts in Hong Kong was being dined out of the officers' mess. This is a quaint old-fashioned habit where an officer who is leaving a posting is essentially the guest at the last formal dinner night before he leaves.

Earlier in my career I had been Mr Vice as the newest and youngest officer in the officers' mess in Münster, but on this occasion I was being bade farewell.

As you might imagine, drink is consumed and, after dinner, foolish games like Mess Rugby can be played, and this night was no exception. Unfortunately, and far more importantly than anything else, Lt General Sir Edwin Bramall was the honoured guest, and after dinner things went slightly wrong. Apparently, and I only have witnesses to verify this, I threw a rugby ball at the general shouting, 'Would you like to play rugby, sir?'

It would have hit him but for the large hand of a Fijian officer called Steve Rabuka who caught it just in time. Steve was a Fijian international prop and had been turning out occasionally for the Army team. He played in the centre for us, and the last thing he said to me that evening was the classical line of, 'Any time you're in Fiji just look me up!'

Fast forward to 1987, and I open my *Daily Telegraph*, and on the front page is a huge photograph of my friend, headlined 'Sitiveni Rabuka takes over after a military coup in Fiji'!

To explain, Mess Rugby is quite easy. There is a room in every officers' mess known as the ante-room which is normally for relaxing in, so it is full of armchairs, and in older messes normally quite large. Imagine a group of twenty or more young officers all dressed in their best evening uniform known as mess kit. Mess Rugby is not dissimilar to Murder Ball that we played at school, only these are fully grown men, the room is full of furniture, and there is no quarter given. I should also add that injuries are frequent, and it is a young man's game, and not for the faint-hearted. Instead of a rugby ball I have played with a cabbage. The try line has been a foot from the wall, so head injuries and concussions almost make modern professional rugby seem safe.

TWENTY-ONE

We do not sit over there

It is May 1974, and the Army has posted me to Pirbright in Surrey, to the Guards Depot, where soldiers belonging to the Household Division were sent to be trained. I was responsible for their dental treatment, and during my time there I can be fairly certain that I did the initial dental inspection for Ian Duncan Smith who for a short time was leader of the Conservative party. That apart, the Guards Depot had a decent reputation in Army rugby circles, so I looked forward to being able to play in regimental matches at a higher level than in Hong Kong.

There was only one problem and that was I couldn't get any of my brother officers to speak to me after my first day. Seating for lunch in the officers' mess was at long tables, with three round tables in the window for the more senior officers. I was told in no uncertain terms by a friend that the table next to the cheese board was where I should sit. 'We do not sit over there', because that was where the civilians, educators, doctors and dentists sat.

After a very good and entertaining lunch on my first day with lots of introductions and chat, my friends from Hong Kong vanished, posted away. Then when I sat in the same place as the previous day, instead of a jolly conversation no one spoke to me. After this had gone on for a couple of weeks I considered moving back to the 'other' table, but I am if nothing stubborn. When a month had gone by it was too late, and the mutterings from the doctors in the medical centre told me I wouldn't be welcome, that I had ideas above my station, and I would never 'fit in' with officers of the Household Division. By and large their officers were normally educated at the UK's top public schools, and this meant they had a language all of their own.

What kept me going was the experience of one of my closest friends from school, Clive Fairweather, who joined the King's Own Scottish Borderers (KOSB) from Sandhurst. As a young officer he had to suffer being ignored for several months, because it was a regimental custom.

Clive went on to command KOSB not just once, but twice. I believe he became one of the longest-serving officers in the SAS, and when he died very sadly a few years ago was described in one obituary as one of Britain's greatest peacetime soldiers.

My feelings were if Clive could stick it out, then so could I. Then one day in mid August a young officer asked me at the lunch table if I thought he would make the rugby team. His name was Neil McCorquodale, a Coldstream Guards officer, who was later to marry Sarah Spencer. His father was regarded as the fastest white man in the world in the 1948 Olympics where he finished fourth in the 100 metres. Neil proved to be blisteringly quick; his only problem was a repeated shoulder dislocation.

His question opened the floodgates, and soon I was the centre of conversations about what kind of team we would have. The answer was not a bad side at all which isn't very surprising when you consider it contained Richard Rea, my old university captain. He was now a medical officer, who was also captaining London Irish. We also had Brian Neck, the Army and Combined Services wing I had played with many times, and a star at Cardiff. There was a well-founded rumour that Brian had lost his place in the Cardiff team to John Bevan because he was playing for the Army, and never got it back because Bevan was then selected for Wales and starred for the Lions.

There were a number of other quality players, many of whom were Welsh Guardsmen, and it took a while to realise that there were several Jones, Davis, Davies and Evans, who were called by their last two numbers. To explain, one Evans was known as '34 Evans', one Davies as '42 Davies', and so on.

We had many memorable matches quite unlike any rugby I had experienced before in the Army. There is nothing quite like the Army Cup for major units.

Regimental rugby in Hong Kong was different to playing for the Royal Army Medical Corps in the UK and playing Army and Combined Services rugby was very different to that again.

The whole of seasons 1974/75 and 1975/76 were all about the major units Army Cup. Over the years this competition has been dominated by 7 Signal Regiment Royal Signals (7 Sigs), 1st Battalion (Bn) Welsh Guards, 1st Bn Duke of Wellington's Regiment, 1st Royal Regiment of Wales (1 RRW), 7th Regiment Royal Horse Artillery (7 RHA).

I have to admit that when I first started working as a dental officer in 1968 I had no idea about regimental pride, until I went to watch the UK major units final between the South Wales Borderers and the Welch Regiment. The only reason I went to watch was because of a player called Tudor Williams who at that time was the Army full back, and I had been told it would be difficult to dislodge him from the team.

At the end of the game, many of the players were in tears as they came off the Aldershot Stadium pitch. Oddly, most of the multitudes of supporters were also very emotional, and I had no idea why until a friend told me that this was the last time the Welch Regiment would play together. It turned out the two regiments were to amalgamate to become the 1st Bn Royal Regiment of Wales, so eighty-eight years of Welch Regiment tradition was vanishing and 280 years of traditions and customs in the South Wales Borderers were being obliterated in the name of military efficiency. Most famously of all it was the South Wales Borderers who defended Rorkes Drift earning eleven Victoria Crosses.

In the twenty-first century the Royal Regiment of Wales amalgamated with the Royal Welch Fusiliers to become the Royal Welsh.

The Duke of Wellingtons' Regiment, a very famous regiment formed in 1702, no longer exists. In December 2004, as part of the reorganisation of the infantry, it was announced that the Duke of Wellington's Regiment would be amalgamated with the Prince of Wales's Own Regiment of Yorkshire and the Green Howards, all Yorkshire-based regiments in the King's Division, to form the Yorkshire Regiment. The Duke's ceased to exist in 2006 after 304 years of history, having won the Army Cup more times than any other infantry regiment at that time. They also had a marvellous international rugby history producing Mike Campbell-Lamerton who captained the Lions in 1966, and Dennis Shuttleworth and Evan Hardy who played half back together for England, to name but three of many.

My research for this book threw up one fact which went to show how the quality of Army rugby in terms of producing internationalists fell. It was to be sixteen years between my first cap in 1969 before the Army had another capped player in 1985. Looking further back, thirty-three Army players were capped in the ten years from 1947, and thirteen capped players between 1957 and 1967, so the numbers dropped dramatically after the end of National Service.

Having said all that, it is very difficult to explain to someone who has never been in the Army exactly what an Army Major

Units Cup match is like. The best way I can describe it is as a cross between two schools in the same town playing a cup match, crossed with Edinburgh versus Glasgow or, in the old days, London Scottish against London Welsh. Defeat is unthinkable, bragging rights almost more important than anything. If the match is between two major rugby playing regiments serving in the same part of the UK, or in BAOR in the early seventies, then the touchlines would be packed and the atmosphere absolutely electric.

My first indirect involvement in regimental rugby had actually happened before I went to Hong Kong in 1971. This was shortly after Scotland had decided my services were no longer required when I had a very mysterious telephone call, asking if I would like to share the radio commentary for the British Forces Broadcasting Service (BFBS) of the final of the UK Army Cup.

That was a shock which turned to absolute delight when the voice said I would be sharing the commentary with none other than the legendary Cliff Morgan. What a thrill to be asked, because Cliff had been one of my heroes from when I was a little boy. I remember seeing him on a grainy film scoring a fantastic individual try for the Lions against the Springboks in 1955.

What was best of all was meeting this god of a man and discovering he was even nicer than I had imagined he would be. We had a very good lunch in the Parachute Brigade officers' mess, and Cliff explained how simple broadcasting on the radio was. He told me we would arrive at the ground, the Aldershot Services ground, about ten minutes before half-time, and when the half-time whistle went he would introduce me, and all I had to do was answer his questions, plus a comment about the first half.

The weather was appalling, and when we arrived at the ground the players were virtually unrecognisable. As I sat next to Cliff awaiting the start of the broadcast as the first half drew to a close, with the score I believe 3–3, he explained about the lip microphone, and the fact that unless it was pressed against my top lip the listeners wouldn't hear what I was saying.

As the half-time whistle went Cliff Morgan introduced himself to the listening audience in BAOR, then I was introduced as the Scottish international full back and Army dentist, finishing with, 'We have just seen a very exciting first half, so I'll hand you over to Ian who will summarise.'

At which point Cliff put down his microphone with the words, 'If you get stuck just say something like, "And what do you think, Cliff?" and I'll come back and help you out.' He followed that with, 'I'm off to the loo.' And with that he disappeared out of the door. This left me, with no programme and thirty unrecognisable players, a score tied at 3–3, and to the best of my knowledge not one player I knew, and a match that had obviously been pretty awful so far. The rain continued to teem down and I somehow or other lasted through the five-minute break, at which time Cliff reappeared with the words, 'I was outside the door in case you got stuck, but there didn't seem to be any danger of that – well done, any time you want a job just call!'

All in all, it had been a remarkable afternoon spent in the company of one of the legends of the game, who proved to be every bit as delightful as he appeared to be.

The Guards Depot were never good enough to win the Major Units Army Cup, the closest we came was being defeated by the Duke of Wellington's Regiment in the UK semi-final.

I do have two very different memories of the cup, one quite worrying, and the other very amusing. In around 1975/76, although I can't be certain exactly when it was, we had to play the Royal Regiment of Wales who at that time were at Holywood Barracks in Belfast. The Troubles in Ulster were not going away, and whilst we weren't that keen to go, there really wasn't any choice.

The journey to the barracks from the airport seemed to be cross country and the bus got stuck behind a tractor with straw bales. I had just seen a movie about the French resistance during the Second World War where the occupants of a similar tractor suddenly kicked over the straw bales to reveal a machine gun, so I had a few bad moments.

We didn't play very well and were duly beaten and, on the way back, the bus broke down near the docks. One of our players hailed a passing cyclist, telling him, 'We're from the barracks.' At this point one of the team said he would run back to the barracks to get help, and John Henderson, a captain in the Welsh Guards, came up to me saying, 'Sir, what do you want us to do?'

John and I were good friends, so I laughed, asking him what all this 'sir' stuff was all about. It turned out I was the senior officer on the bus as a major and I would be held responsible if anything happened. Apparently if the cyclist had been an IRA sympathiser then they could come back with weapons and start shooting. Anyway, taking his advice we hid, or perhaps cowered would be more accurate, behind some gorse bushes until a replacement bus arrived!

On another occasion, the Guards Depot played the Army Air Corps with a hurricane wind blowing up and down the pitch. We lost the toss and were forced to take the wind in the first half. Unbelievably I dropped a goal from around our twenty-five-yard line, which was still rising as it crossed the bar! Our players jumped around, cheered, shouted things like 'great kick', 'fantastic' and ran backwards to get ready for the kick-off. The poor referee was so pressured by this because he really didn't have a clue. I don't suppose he'd ever seen anyone stupid enough to try something like that, so he awarded the drop goal.

The wind was so bad you couldn't pass when it was behind you, and you couldn't kick running into it, or get a lineout throw straight. It was without a doubt the worst conditions I had ever played in.

My old friend Richard Rea was at scrum half and in the second half we had all the lineout ball because they couldn't throw straight. All he then did was to just run at them. At fly half I didn't get one pass after half-time, plus the fact they won not one single ball, and we won this epic 3–0!

On another occasion we played RMCS Shrivenham, in a match that almost had fatal consequences. We were using a variation on the wall penalty move described earlier. Our version was to pass the ball back to a forward who was hidden ten yards behind the middle of the wall, and he would run and a player would step out of the wall and he would slip through. Our chosen man was 'Zeb' Spring of the Coldstream Guards. Unfortunately, the opposition had set a man off to run at the wall to try to win a penalty for obstruction and he and Zeb met head on like two cars in a collision. The sound of bone and flesh colliding was horrible, and whilst no serious damage was done, we didn't do it again!

TWENTY-TWO

I'd like you to accompany
me to the police station

These are not the words any of us likes to hear, especially when you are an officer in the Royal Army Dental Corps. Being arrested under any circumstances and being potentially charged with malicious damage could have brought not only my army career crashing down but also have me struck off the dental register.

It all happened during season 1975/76 when the Guards Depot rugby team went on tour to Wales. We played Maesteg Celtic, the result of the game having vanished into the mists of time and has been overshadowed by what happened after the match.

I can't quite remember, but something seemed to have happened to their clubhouse, and they had lost all their memorabilia, such as old jerseys, caps, ties, that sort of thing. I was wearing my Scotland player's tie which I handed over to them to start a new collection, and somehow or other ended up wearing two Maesteg Celtic ties.

So far so good, it was on the way back to the team bus in town that the problem occurred. Drunken memories of my colonel in Hong Kong and going down streets without touching the ground by climbing over cars meant that this was exactly what I did. The difficulty I found myself in occurred because one of the cars I was climbing over had a plastic roof, and through it I went!

Seconds after I got back on our team bus two police officers appeared and the fateful words were uttered. Off we went, and very shortly afterwards I found myself in the police inspector's office. According to the member of the team who went with me for moral support, I sat slouched in a chair with my feet on the desk, and unaware of the mess I was in.

I was about to be charged when the inspector noticed my outfit and asked me what I was doing wearing two Maesteg ties. It was then he remembered he had been in the rugby club earlier when there was a bit of a fuss about the tie presentation and the penny dropped. The Welsh match in 1971 and the Gerald Davies try caused him much mirth! All I can say is thank goodness.

The driver of the car was sent for and when he arrived, very much the worse for wear, the police inspector offered him the choice of me offering to pay £30 for the damage or I could be charged. Very angrily he insisted I was charged, which was when the police inspector asked him if he was the driver of the car and invited him to take a breath test. Naturally he accepted my offer, and I luckily walked out a free man. It would be fair to say that discipline the next day at training was slightly tricky!

Although I was now a long way physically and mentally from the rugby player I was in 1971, as four years had passed, I was still to experience the first-class game just once more under somewhat unusual circumstances.

Richard Rea and I had been friends since our early days at university and in 1968 on New Year's Day I had been staying with the Rea family in Belfast and played in a crazy game of rugby for the North of Ireland Wednesday Club. It was supposed to be a friendly and I was playing on the wing. I kept being flattened by this aggressive Irishman in a distinctly unfriendly manner. After the game he congratulated me saying he had never come across a wing who tackled and kicked with both feet!

Richard then told me I had been marking the legendary Mike Gibson. Imagine a Lions star or, for that matter, any professional rugby star playing in a New Year's Day friendly these days. It would never happen.

Fast forward to 1975, and Richard asked me if I would turn out at fly half for a London Irish XV thinly disguised as 'Mick Molloy's XV' to play at Havant in Hampshire. I absolutely loved it, managed to drop a goal, and just to play with first-team players in a senior club again was such a treat. Little did I know what was to follow.

London Irish had taken somewhat of a hammering just before Easter and were having a problem raising a side to travel to Bridgend on Good Friday evening to play under the lights. Richard asked me if I would play for them at fly half. My initial response was that I couldn't because I was Scottish, and at that time there was no way a Scotsman would – or could – turn out for another of the Exiles teams. Richard's comment was, 'You learned your rugby in Ireland'.

When asked how that was possible, I discovered that playing for North Wednesday Club on New Year's Day 1968 automatically qualified me to play for London Irish! I agreed to play under a pseudonym in case any press reporters were there, with a good Irish name like O'Farrell.

We lost a man fairly early on and, with no substitutes, it was very much a game of box-kicking and trying to keep the pack moving forwards. To be honest, I didn't know what a box-kick was at that stage. My attempts at an up-and-under failed lamentably, as even my best high kick downwind was beautifully caught by the Bridgend full back off his fingertips and kicked back over my head into the wind with a beautiful touch-finder.

We somehow managed to stay in the game, which was a miracle, and it was only afterwards in the bar that I discovered the rugby correspondent for the *Western Mail* was at the match. Apparently, he asked who the Irish fly half was, and being told it was O'Farrell, said he didn't think so. Eventually he exclaimed, 'That's Ian Smith the former Scotland full back,' as he had seen my left foot before. He was asked not to put that in his article, and if he had to mention the fly half his name was O'Farrell.

The reporter was the legendary Carwyn James, coach of Llanelli and, most famously, the '71 Lions – and O'Farrell got a good write-up!

I was then asked if I'd like to play at fly half for London Irish during the next season, but I felt my time had gone, and I really didn't see myself turning out against London Scottish.

That was definitely the end of my first class rugby career, but I was still to have the grim experience of being on the receiving end of an ex-Newport flanker.

TWENTY-THREE

He's too dirty to play for Newport, so we have to pick him

In terms of a life playing rugby being described as a match, I am now deep into the last quarter, with the only difference being at this stage, in 1976, I don't know how long there is left before the final whistle.

Berlin was to be my service rugby swansong that year, and it provided me with two totally different experiences. I drove to Berlin through East Germany, which was an eye-opener, because the autobahn appeared not to have been touched since 1945 – it had grass growing on parts of it, and recognisable shell holes still pocked the tarmac.

As part of the British garrison, and I was working in the British Military Hospital, we were technically still on rations as a leftover from the Berlin airlift after the Second World War. This meant, in effect, that we ordered our meat at hugely subsidised prices, so it was possible to eat fillet steak every day if you so wished because you could easily afford it. The British had their own currency known as British Armed Forces Special Vouchers (BAFSV) which could only be used in military shops like the NAAFI.

All the Allied sectors could easily be visited and were a joy because the French had the Economat where you could buy superb cheeses and other French delicacies, whilst the PX sold spirits on a voucher system very cheaply indeed.

East Berlin could only be entered in uniform passing through the legendary Checkpoint Charlie, and of course the Russian Sector was hidden behind the infamous Berlin Wall; in fact the whole city was sealed in by walls and barbed wire.

I found the atmosphere a bit claustrophobic, but rugby was still playing a part in my life. BMH Berlin ran a rugby team of sorts, called the Berlin Bears, and during the short time I spent there I played at scrum half. The main reason for this was it guaranteed I'd see the ball – if only to put it into the set scrums, because it was extremely doubtful I'd ever get it at fly half!

We had an awful struggle to raise a XV; however, the team spirit was amazing, and the games, whilst enjoyable, were not without risk to life and limb, as I found myself to be a target. How lucky I was to have one or two players 'riding shotgun' and protecting me from boots and fists. I really enjoyed my time with the team, and realising my rugby was coming to an end at a very similar level to my experiences with BMH Münster made it all the better. I really felt as if the circle of my rugby life was virtually complete.

The Welsh Guards then asked me to play for them, as I was technically their dental officer, against a Welsh valley side who were on tour. This was a substantially higher standard as the Welsh Guards were then, and remain so, one of the top rugby-playing major units in the British Army. To say the match was very competitive is to say the least. This is just a polite way of saying it was brutally violent!

At one point I was trapped in a maul with the ball, my arms were trapped by my side, and then I became aware of two thumbs in my eyes. I screamed very loudly, or loudly enough for the referee to blow his whistle. He saw the scratches to my eyes and awarded us a penalty.

I'd never really been scared for my personal safety on a rugby pitch until that point, but I felt I had come fairly close to serious eye damage, and I was not at all keen to get caught in possession again.

In the bar after the game one of their side came up to me and told me how lucky I was. He told me not only had he attempted to gouge my eyes, but he had tried to jump on my knee when I was on the ground, to, as he put it nicely, get me off the pitch.

I took him over to one of their committee and told them what he had said, adding that there was no way this man should ever be allowed on a rugby pitch again.

His response was, 'He's too dirty to play for Newport, so we have to pick him.'

If that is what rugby in the Welsh valleys in 1977 was like, I was very glad to be leaving the army, and settling down in west Norfolk, once again promising Maureen that this really was the end of my rugby career.

TWENTY-FOUR

The final whistle

When my wife and I first arrived in East Anglia the local rugby club, West Norfolk, based in nearby King's Lynn, asked if I might help out with training. I was more than happy to do this but was quite horrified at the total lack of ball use. Training seemed to consist of endless running up and down the pitch, press-ups, but nothing very creative at all. In fact, much the way it was when I had been at school in the late fifties. Over a few weeks we persuaded every player to obtain a rugby ball, so that all the running around that they did was with a ball in hand. It was only a small thing, but it did make a difference. Training always ended with unopposed drills, and on one or two occasions I filled in at fly half, with no real intentions of playing.

I had become friendly with a local farmer, Simon Thompson, who like myself was getting a bit old for serious rugby, so, much to my wife's disgust, I started to turn out for the seconds. One reason was that there were words I could say to a young player at training about what he should do, and where he should position himself, but showing is always better than telling. Simon and I agreed we would play fly half and centre.

I was introduced recently by Mark Ballman, the president of West Norfolk RFC, at a pre-match lunch as: 'Ian Smith who played for Edinburgh University, Heriot's FP, London Scottish, Hampshire, the Army, Combined Services, Scotland, and our 2nds, as we never considered Ian good enough for the firsts!'

West Norfolk play their rugby normally in London 3 Eastern Counties, which if you are English might give you an idea at the level they play. To put it into perspective it is the eighth level of competitive rugby in England. Quite where that places the 2nd XV is a matter for conjecture!

There is nothing at all wrong with that, in fact I am proud to say my last game of rugby was for the West Norfolk 2nd XV. It was twenty-nine years after I started my school rugby career in the 36th and bottom team in the school so I finished where I started, at a low level.

I regard that as a circle completed, and to describe it in another way it is like starting at the bottom of the mountain and trying to climb to the top. I didn't quite make the summit which has to be selection for the Lions, but at least I got to within touching distance, without having the ability to go the rest of the way.

Playing international rugby wasn't too bad an achievement, but the reverse trip to West Norfolk 2nd XV gave me a far better insight into what makes rugby such a great game, than if I had listened to my wife in 1971 and retired completely! The few games I played for the 2nd XV at West Norfolk gave me a huge amount of pleasure, and how I wish it could have continued for longer.

There is no shame in becoming an ageing player, and to be able to be just a little bit of help to an eighteen-year-old taking his first nervous steps into adult rugby.

I can still remember playing at Heriot's Former Pupils as a teenager, just after leaving school, sitting in a dressing room with three or four players who were puffing on cigarettes, a couple of others taping themselves up like an Egyptian mummy, and almost without exception the older players smothering themselves in liniment. None of which I understood!

There was no question of the 3rd XV going out to warm up, they needed all their energy for the match ahead! The wise old sage sitting next to me warned me about their dirty inside centre who tackled late and high, and advised me not to get into a ruck when their number eight was around because he trampled and if I got caught in a maul he might go for my eyes. Thank God these practices have disappeared almost entirely from the game.

The words of encouragement when I did something good from a prop I'd watched play for the 1sts meant more to me than he would ever realise. When my turn came to be a veteran, I never felt it was giving back. I hate that expression – it was much more passing on hard-won experience. It was so much easier to show than to tell when it came to playing the game, and a pat on the back to a youngster was simply repeating what had happened to me all those years before.

I think Simon and I only played twice together for the West Norfolk 2nd XV, and then the committee told us that it had to stop, which was sad. The thing is that as time goes by rugby clubs are not immune to change and what had been very much a local farmers and old boys club was becoming much more inclusive, and what a good thing that was. New and dedicated committee men like Charlie Curtis and Pat Wakefield, amongst others, were driving the club forward in a different direction, and this meant some friction with the older members, which was the situation that had boiled over in the early eighties. To be fair, I was by then even slower than your average prop, although physically hardly a shadow of my former self! I hadn't been much good on the coaching front either as I could never watch the team play on a Saturday unless it was in the school holidays.

The reason for this was, not only did we have another son, Matthew, who was still very small, I had no intention of repeating my failures as a father between 1969 and 1971. Also my two older boys, Simon and Mark, were both away at a boarding preparatory school called Glebe House in Hunstanton on the north Norfolk coast. We chose this school because it had an outstanding rugby record, which to me was more important than anything else!

How different life was then, because my two little boys went straight into full-time boarding aged eight. As parents we weren't allowed to visit for the first two weeks, and the only time we got to see them was after church on a Sunday, and after matches on Wednesdays and Saturdays. Even then we got perhaps thirty minutes together in the car before the bell rang and they had to go. It seems in the twenty-first century almost medieval, but we felt it was important for them to be educated there.

What was really impressive was the standard of rugby played by the 1st XV, who were mainly twelve- and early-thirteen-year-olds. The skill levels not only of the Glebe House boys were very high, but also the other schools, most of whom Glebe House beat.

The master in charge of rugby was a man called Richard Brearley. He was still very young at the time, and I think it may have been his first job after qualifying at Borough Road College. He really did understand small boys, and how to get the very best out of them.

Richard eventually moved from Glebe House to Greshams School in Holt, where he has to take a huge amount of credit for developing the talents of England international stars Ben and Tom Youngs.

This background actually set the scene for my last two games of rugby, both of which ended in total humiliation.

Firstly, Richard asked me if I would play for the Headmaster's XV against the Greshams Senior School 1st XV in Holt, Norfolk.

The Headmaster, one Logie Bruce-Lockhart, remains a legend. An armoured car commander in the Second World War, he won five caps for Scotland and then spent the next decades as headmaster at Greshams. It was a huge privilege not only to be asked to play for his side, but also to meet him.

I wouldn't say the match was a complete disaster, but when the three-quarters, Duncan Bruce-Lockhart, Nick Chesworth – both of whom played high-level first-class rugby – and Richard Brearley had to stand still to wait to pass to me when I came into the line, I knew it was final whistle time.

The final embarrassment lay just around the corner while playing for West Norfolk 2nd XV on a back pitch. We were captained by a redoubtable Welshman, Peter Brennan, in the forwards and featuring myself at fly half I made a fundamental error of judgement, for which I blame my rugby masters at school, Donald Hastie and Donald McIntyre.

I still remember the shout from Donald Hastie right at the beginning of my playing days at school. 'Alexander you turned your back on the ball after I awarded that penalty, another ten yards, Blues.' You jolly quickly learned to back-pedal facing the ball when a penalty was awarded against your team.

Therefore, I have taken a huge number of tap-and-go penalties over the years when the opposition have turned their backs after a penalty has been awarded against them.

That was all very well when I was young, fit and still with a reasonable turn of speed, but to do it when unfit is just plain stupid. In no time you become isolated as you have taken the penalty so quickly, so you then need to be able to outrun any opposition who have woken up to what you are doing.

Well of course this is exactly what happened to this ageing full back, pretending to be a fly half. We were awarded a penalty on our ten-metre line, and the opposition turned round and jogged away.

Before I could stop myself I had tapped the ball and started running. Very quickly I had gone past their retreating players and to my horror realised I still had forty yards to run. The closer I got to the line, the more I could see out of the corner of my eye one of my opponents running to cut me off. I mistakenly thought about ten yards out I could neatly step inside him, but my legs buckled, I head-butted him in the stomach and staggered over the line. As the referee, former Scottish international Bob Steven, arrived on the scene, I was sick all over his boots!

How ignominious, but how fitting in a very real sense that Donald Hastie was there at the beginning and at the very end.

Then the final whistle blew . . .

AFTERWORD

View from the clubhouse

It's a sad fact that during a rugby career, if you are lucky enough to be playing top-class rugby and hoping you can go even further in the game, that you probably give little thought to those players in the junior sides.

I know this kind of attitude is selfish, but you are selfish because you are focused on your own goals. What this can mean is that you will be training and practising with the top players in your club, probably changing in a different dressing room, so your contact with the players in the lower sides is limited.

Today many top players will never experience the joys of junior rugby because they have been identified as having talent at a very early stage and spend their rugby careers in the top teams. Let me explain more fully what I mean by this.

Many of today's pro players started out in the Minis on a Sunday morning at a junior club. When they got to their early teens they were selected to be coached by their nearest pro club – in our case, in West Norfolk, that would be Leicester.

I remember attending a selection morning for what eventually would be the Leicester Academy one Sunday with our son

Alexander. What happened was the parents were all spoken to as a group, told not to raise our hopes, and that non-selection wasn't the end of the world. In fact the children were just at the base of a very large pyramid with only very few capable of reaching the apex which would be playing for Leicester.

It was interesting to be told by one of the coaches that the real reason for getting us all together was to look at how big the parents were. Children of very tall parents with a modicum of ability would be chosen because of their potential size, and the children of parents with a rugby pedigree would also be chosen.

It is here that the separation begins, because quite quickly the chosen few start playing matches at Leicester, a few go on to the likes of the Leicester Academy, and right from the start they are banned from playing at their local club. Their diet is controlled, a strict training regime is introduced and eventually some will have to move schools and move to Leicester as well, taking them away from their friendship group.

In the early stages I remember being told that Alexander would have to attend judo classes as well as the other training programmes. This just seemed a bit too much for a young teenager who also played decent hockey and who, like his father, wanted to experience all kinds of sports, and not have to sacrifice all for just one. The last straw came when he went to his senior school and was told that three sessions a week in the gym would be required.

Recently I attended a Leicester versus Gloucester match and in the programme were photographs of the members of the Leicester development squad. I recognised one of the players who had been a very talented fly half as a youngster at West Norfolk. His photograph described him as a hooker with what looked like a nineteen-inch collar size. I just wondered, in amazement, how many gym sessions a week it took to produce this physique and was it all worth it.

At some stage there will, of course, be many players who are not good enough, some suffer injuries, many are quite unceremoniously dumped, and a few make it. Not many young men who were deemed excess to requirements return to their original clubs, which is very understandable, as pride plays a large part here. Sadly, this very often means they are lost to the game.

There are parents who honestly believe their child has the talent to succeed, and despite their son not making the grade at, say, Leicester take them to another senior club and they go on to have great success. One such case at West Norfolk was with a parent called Wally Price who, on being told his son, Ali, wasn't going to make it at one club, simply moved him. The rest is history as Ali is arguably, at the time of writing, the best scrum half in Scotland, playing for Glasgow Warriors and has twenty-four caps and counting, whilst being spoken of as a possible Lion.

This whole process takes players away from their roots in the game. The question is what happens next when their time at one of the top clubs comes to an end, as age takes its toll?

In many respects it is a tragedy that most pro and international players announce their retirement at the top, and never play again. Very few slowly go back down through the levels, and while I hate to use the words 'giving back to the game', they would certainly do that, as well as getting the huge pleasure to be had from 'playing down'.

Perhaps one reason is that they have no home club anymore. It is all very well to be a Leicester or a Wasps player, but where do you play when that part of your rugby life is over? I can understand players may simply be burnt out, having played far too much rugby. Sadly there isn't really anywhere for them to go on playing if they want to and are able, because they effectively left their home club as a young teenager. What this means is they have lost touch so miss out on being able to play social rugby with the mates they have grown up with, played with, trained with, had fun with, and then being able to hand on their experience to the youngsters coming through.

When I was young, in the fifties and sixties, players were selected to play for their country from a club side. The normal route was club junior side, club 1st XV, district, international trial, international cap. When it was decided your time as an international was up, then you made the journey in reverse, and happily so. Some clubs ran up to ten teams, and it was the slow decline amongst friends and playing against old friends, some of whom had been on the same journey. As a young man, you played against opponents who had become friends, then drank and socialised together after the match. As a veteran you carried this on except you might well go out for supper with friends who were opponents, only now you are joined by your wives who had also become friends.

This was the nice way to wind down a rugby career. That situation no longer exists. As an aging player gradually declining in speed, with perhaps commensurate lowering of skill levels, the invaluable experience you have had of top-class rugby can allow you to still look good and, better than that, feel good. Best of all, the tension, the sick feeling in the pit of your stomach before games as you are trying desperately hard to make your club 1st XV, district, provincial or international team, and know you are being closely watched by selectors, newspaper reporters and television commentators, who will be quick to praise, but even quicker to criticise, has disappeared forever.

The lower level you play and the older you get, the more your teammates look after you, as if you were a piece of fine bone china that might easily break. They are quite correct, injury recovery is slower, warm-ups take longer, but you have learned from bitter experience how to conserve your energy. Best of all you still have the ability, experience and knowledge to put that to best use for the team without worrying about your personal performance.

The other side of the coin is sadly and all too often injury or family pressures end a playing career, when still young enough to go on playing, so young men – and not so young men – miss out on the heart and soul of rugby in the lower teams, and the junior clubs, where Michael Green's *The Art of Coarse Rugby* still hold sway.

We must never forget that without the unheralded and unsung players in the lower sides and junior clubs, there would be no rugby at the top level. Every pyramid must have a base, and the wider that base the higher the top can be.

It would have been incredibly sad for me never to have experienced my last eleven or twelve years of lower-grade rugby during which I was extremely fortunate to be relatively injury free and thus able to enjoy it fully.

I do understand that the game of rugby has become a great deal more brutal in the past few years. Full-time professionalism and the sheer size and speed of the modern top-class rugby player is quite frightening. If you ever stand alongside one of the giants of the game today you get to realise just how massive they are.

Collisions have meant a dramatic increase in serious injuries, and the number of first-class players who will never play again, whilst still comparatively young is very sad. This also explains why you don't find many, if any, former internationals playing down at junior club 2nd XV level today. One major reason is that many are crippled and, if not when they give up playing professionally, then certainly later.

Comparisons between players can be irrelevant because memories of days gone by can play tricks, and the 'rugby gods' from the sixties and seventies may never have survived the physicality of modern-day rugby.

Nevertheless, as I cast my now less than reliable memory back to my schooldays and university days, when George Heriot's 1st XV were the best school team in Scotland and Edinburgh University spent ninety-five per cent of seasons 1966/67 and 1967/68 as the leading first-class side in Scotland, there is one memory that stands out. That memory is the almost total lack of serious injuries. In my school 1st XV, over three seasons, there was only one long-term injury and in the university side I can't remember anyone missing more than a couple of weeks, and not one career-ending or really serious injury. If this was to be compared with the Stowe School 1st XV, where my children were educated, in season 2015/16 at half-term in October around half the side were unavailable with serious injuries.

Looking at the injuries plaguing England prior to the autumn internationals in 2018, or the training injuries suffered by their squad members, the sheer scale of it would terrify me if I were a player today. If I were the parent of a youngster wanting a professional career in rugby I wouldn't be too happy.

I can honestly say, that nervous as I was before a game, it was never fear of injury that bothered me, only a fear of playing badly and letting my team and myself down. Afterwards I had to go home and face a very critical father.

I have been incredibly lucky in that I was able to play rugby at most levels without my playing career being shortened by injury. There seems hardly a week that goes by without some player announcing his premature retirement from the game.

If I look back to the time when I played, first-class rugby players, almost without exception, played for one club throughout their careers, never received a penny, sometimes were capped by their country, returned to their clubs, and then played down through the club lending their invaluable experience to youngsters on the way up. There were no overseas players, or very few playing club rugby in the UK.

I well remember Bob Hiller, one of England's greatest full backs, playing for Harlequins 3rd XV as one example of what happened a lot of the time when I was a young player. How sad that seems to have gone, and by that I mean club 3rd XVs as much as anything.

You might ask therefore what's so great about playing for thirty-five different teams throughout my playing career – and how did that happen anyway? The answer is simple in that I was in the British Army and was therefore posted from Edinburgh to Germany, to England, to Hong Kong, to England, to Berlin, to West Germany, and then finally to live and work in west Norfolk. I never had the joy of rising to the 1st XV in one club, then gaining representative honours, followed by slowly going down to the junior XVs, and I really wish it had been like that.

When I was struggling with my rugby career and playing for London Scottish Extra A (3rds) in 1969, we went to Guildford and Godalming rugby club. If my hazy memory has got the club wrong, I apologise, but I am certain the clubhouse had a thatched roof, and my outstanding memory was of the wives and girlfriends doing match teas, and the atmosphere of togetherness. It made me wish I belonged to a club like that where you could always be amongst the friends you grew up with.

If this sounds like sentimental codswallop I don't apologise because with the advent of leagues even for junior clubs some of this has been lost.

No longer are ancient rivalries enjoyed because of promotion and relegation in the modern league structure, which means teams change divisions and therefore change who they play against year on year. My local club, West Norfolk, spent some seasons, thanks to the leagues, playing in north and east London, Mersea Island, Canvey Island and other parts of darkest Essex. That is at least a two-hour drive there and back to play opponents you have no history with, no friendships to rekindle, just things like dog dirt all over one north London pitch. No more regular fixtures against Norwich, North Walsham, Diss and Holt, who with many others were ancient rivals. Was it any wonder that even the 1st XV could struggle to produce twenty-three players for such a long journey with little joy at the end?

In fairness, at the time of writing, West Norfolk's fixtures in London 3 Eastern Counties are more local, but should promotion be won then this could mean a return to long-distance fixtures.

I fear something intangible has been lost at the lower levels of rugby forever. The success or failure of national sides depends totally on the health of the game at the bottom of the pyramid. The evidence available would indicate that leagues and promotion and relegation have reduced the number of teams fielded by clubs at the junior level. It is time that the administrators of the game found a solution before it is too late.

POSTSCRIPT

Teams

1. George Heriot's School – 1953–63
2. Edinburgh Schools – 1962–63
3. Scottish Schools 1963 (cancelled)
4. Edinburgh University – 1964–68
5. Scottish Universities – 1967
6. North of Ireland Wednesday Club – 1968
7. Co-Optimists – 1968–69
8. Heriot's FP – 1968
9. British Military Hospital Münster – 1968
10. Royal Green Jackets – 1968
11. BAOR Probables XV – 1968
12. BAOR XV – 1968
13. British Army – 1968–71
14. London Scottish – 1969–71
15. Combined Services – 1969–71
16. Scottish Rugby Trial Blues XV
17. Scotland Rugby Trial Probables (Scotland vs the Rest) XV
18. Royal Military Academy Sandhurst Commandant's XV – 1969
19. RAMC – 1969–71

20. Bosuns – 1970
21. Hampshire – 1969–71
22. Aldershot Services – 1971
23. Army Hong Kong – 1971–74
24. 51 Brigade Hong Kong – 1972–74
25. 1st Bn Irish Guards – 1971–73
26. 1 Kings – 1973–74
27. Combined Services Hong Kong – 1972–74
28. Taipans XV – 1972
29. Commander British Forces XV – 1973
30. Hong Kong – 1972–74
31. Hong Kong Co-Optimists – 1972–74
32. Guards Depot Pirbright – 1974–76
33. London Irish – 1975
34. British Military Hospital Berlin – 1976–77
35. Welsh Guards – 1977
36. Greshams Headmasters XV – 1981
37. West Norfolk 2nd XV – 1981

ACKNOWLEDGEMENTS

This account would never have been written if it hadn't been for a good friend Ian Hay who picked up the book *Behind the Thistle* in an Edinburgh bookshop a few years ago. To my surprise I found my photograph on one of the pages, and this introduced me to my publishers, Arena Sport.

I have to thank them, especially Peter Burns the Sports Editor, for reading my drafts and feeling there was enough interest to publish. The amount of work that goes into publishing staggers me, and I need to thank everyone involved at Arena who guided me through all the hard work it entails

I must thank my late parents for the sacrifices they made, their support and encouragement to allow me to follow my dream to play for Scotland. In particular, thanks must go to my father for his enthusiastic collecting of press cuttings without which this book would not have been possible.

I owe much to my late wife Maureen, who had to play second fiddle to my rugby. She allowed me to abandon her with more than one baby whilst I went away to play. She was very patient when I kept retiring and then changing my mind. How she managed to cope I do not know.

Very special thanks to Julie my wife, who found the press cuttings and pressured me to write it all down for my grandchildren. Without her love and insistence this book would never have been written.

Thanks also to my old friends Alastair Brown, who unknowingly made me realise I could write, Peter Brennan, my last rugby captain, and his wife Anita, who worked very hard to correct my very poor grammar. Finally, Tony Hogarth my school 1st XV captain, and very old friend, who made me believe my rugby story was interesting.

Ian Smith, 2019